Rock and Vine
Next Generation Changemakers in America's Wine Country

Library of Congress Catalog Number pending
ISBN Number: 978-0-615-69119-0

Design by: Gabe Ruane
Consulting Editor: Christy Canterbury, Master of Wine
Copy Editor: Paula Dragosh

Printed in China
Non-Fiction

City of Publication: San Francisco, CA

Authored by: Chelsea Prince
Photography by: Mary Steinbacher

Chelsea Print & Publishing is an aesthetically-focused publishing company with a commitment to modern storytelling, accessible professional art and the support of non-profits related to its published works.

Chelsea
print & publishing

rockandvinebook.com
chelseaprintandpublishing.com

Acknowledgements

The idea for *Rock and Vine* was inspired by a wine tasting event in San Francisco featuring Ben Flajnik and Envolve Winery. Ben was the first person to say "yes" to this book. Thank you.

I deeply thank everyone profiled in this book for your trust, time, enthusiasm and friendship. I am honored to know you. I hope you all look back on this book years from now with fond memories of your early successes.

Mary Steinbacher, your positivity is contagious. We worked day in and day out together for six months, and you chose to be joyful throughout it all. Your spirit eminates throughout this book.

Gabe Ruane, you are the epitome of talent. Thank you for your continued partnership, and for entertaining my wild ideas.

Christy Canterbury, MW. You are a blessing.

Others: Copy editor Paula Dragosh, Liz Grennan, Dennis Kelly, Mimi Toro, Shannon Staglin, Paul Roberts, Rhadhika Dutt, Philip James, Janet Thomas, Jim Knapp, Mary Grace, Amy Field, Hal Belmont, and my family.

"With man this is impossible, but with God all things are possible." Mathew 19:26

Publisher's Note

The wine professionals profiled in *Rock and Vine* were chosen at the discretion of the publisher. The publisher sought out peer references and conducted extensive research to determine each candidate's character, potential influence on the wine industry, and suitability for the book. The publisher did not choose any persons above the age of 35.

Each generation discovers for itself the character of place in the context of time. Each individual does the same. That process is inexorable—and inseparable from the land, for gravity grounds us all.

- H. WILLIAM HARLAN

ROCK AND VINE

Next Generation Changemakers
in America's Wine Country

The next generation of California wine professionals has arrived.

The first party of influential vintners arrived in the 1970s and 80s through the personalities of Robert and Peter Mondavi, Joel Peterson, Mike Benziger, Don Sebastiani and Chuck Wagner. Those were the pioneer days, when winemakers staged the first announcements of Napa's and Sonoma's might. Then came the 1990s, and California wines rose to fame. Wine became fancier, winemakers became icons, and American wine was rightfully acknowledged by the world.

The children and grandchildren of these trailblazers have matured and are crafting their own convivial brands with less pomp and better circumstances. *Rock and Vine* showcases eleven profiles enhanced by unforgettable portrait and vineyard photography representing the Grand Cru of wine industry millennials in Napa and Sonoma.

Contents

Introduction

Establishing New Vines

Envolve Winery *BEN FLAJNIK, MIKE BENZIGER, DANNY FAY*
BNA Wine Group *TONY LEONARDINI*
Free Flow Wines *JORDAN KIVELSTADT*

Q&A *PAUL ROBERTS Master Sommelier, Bond Estates*

Harvesting the New Crop of Talent

Futo *JASON EXPOSTO*
Far Niente *NICOLE MARCHESI*

Q&A *SHANNON STAGLIN Staglin Family Vineyards*

Family Roots Digging Deeper

Ceja Vineyards *DALIA CEJA*
Wagner Family Made Wine *JOE WAGNER*
Turley Wine Cellars *CHRISTINA TURLEY*

Q&A: *DENNIS KELLY Master Sommelier, The French Laundry*

Transitioning into New Clones

Bedrock Wine *MORGAN TWAIN-PETERSON*
The Other Guys *AUGUST SEBASTIANI*
Dark Matter *ANGELINA MONDAVI*

Q&A: *JAMES PHILIP Lot 18*

Introduction

MAGGIE PRAMUK
Robert Biale Vineyards

It's funny what kind of twists and turns can happen on a creative project such as *Rock and Vine*. I met Chelsea during the course of her research on *Rock and Vine*, and we instantly connected. This intuitive and prescient publisher has tuned in to a current subject that is a hot topic in California — Where is the California wine industry going? Who is going to take over for the passionate entrepreneurs who started wineries in the 1970s, 80s and 90s?

Industry surveys and analyses indicate that nearly half of California's wineries are going to change hands in the next several years. As corporations continue to buy out boutique and iconic wineries, these issues will come to the forefront. Meanwhile, wineries still owned by families are experiencing a changing of the guard, so to speak. The legacy of Napa and Sonoma will carry on—that's for sure—but it's those special innovators in our midst who will enhance it.

I'm proud to say that I personally know many of the men and women chosen for this book. I consider them friends and colleagues, and I know we share many of the same joys and challenges in this wonderful, and sometimes crazy, agricultural business. Chelsea has taken quality time to get to know all of us personally; she understands our ambitions and values, and visualizes our potential. The resulting book is a veritable reflection and important statement about the future of Napa and Sonoma and its devoted wine advocates.

If someone asked me ten years ago where I saw myself when I was 25, I would not have said I'd be living in the Napa Valley and working side by side with my dad at my family's winery. I thought I would be living in a big city far away from Napa, the little town I grew up in. I was fifteen then, so what did I know? Now I can't see myself anywhere else other than where I'm working today, at Robert Biale Vineyards.

I started in the wine industry when I was six, happily stuffing and stamping envelopes for my dad and his best friend Bob, oblivious to what was really going on. Little did I know they were starting their winery, out of a garage. Now, I'm working for the very same company (occasionally still stuffing envelopes), and Robert Biale Vineyards is one of the world's leading producers of Zinfandel.

My dad and Bob started with one wine made from Bob's parents' vineyard, and today Robert Biale Vineyards produces 24 different wines, 14 of those being Zinfandels. Our wines are sourced from some of the oldest vineyards in California. Our mission and passion is to preserve California's heritage vineyards and to teach people about the uniqueness of site-driven wines. I fell in love with Biale for so many reasons, but mainly because of my appreciation for how hard, yet rewarding, this job is.

My interest in wine began when I was an undergraduate at San Diego State University. I started cooking continuously my senior year, and gradually started pairing wines with my meals. To test different pairings, I explored neighborhood grocery stores and chatted with its wine specialists; they were always eager to share their knowledge. My recreational curiosity for wine developed into a passion, and after graduation I moved back to Napa to learn about wine in a professional context.

When people ask me what I do at the winery I tell them "everything". My official roles at Biale are Wine Club Coordinator and Marketing Assistant, but my responsibilities stretch far beyond my titles. In the morning I am the Wine Club Coordinator; a few hours later I'm a tour guide; at lunch, I'm tasting samples; and the next day, I am on a plane with my dad headed out to make sales calls with our distributors. During harvest, you can find me standing on the sorting belt, stomping grapes or shoveling out tanks - I've never been afraid to get dirty!

My dad always told me that one doesn't have to know everything about wine to be able to enjoy it. We appreciate wine for the same reason we appreciate fine cuisine: it is social, it gives people something to talk about, and it brings people together. Thousands of years ago it did the same thing - it brought people together. Today, people can build relationships and find community through multiple platforms, which makes wine less intimidating and easier to learn about. My generation started drinking wine at a younger age than my parents' generation because of how accessible it has become.

The next generation of winemakers is taking advantage of new innovations in all aspects of the industry: vineyard management, winemaking and marketing - and mixing them with old techniques. We are combining what has worked for hundreds of years, what we learned from our parents, and modern practices throughout the whole winemaking process. At Biale, and all throughout the industry, winemakers are pushing to protect the land by using environmentally friendly methods to grow grapes and make wine. A hundred years ago, before industrialization, farming was organic; now we're circling back with sustainable dry farming with an emphasis on quality.

So much of the wine industry is about relationships, the people we know and the friends we make. We are all here because we love the culture. We get to be creative, spend time outside and work with the land. At Biale, we share our vineyards with many other producers. We share marketing ideas and even winemaking techniques. As producers in California, we want to help distinguish California as a premiere growing region in the world. Today, there are so many different wines coming from different places around the world, and we work to distinguish California and Napa Valley in particular, as truly world class.

There are so many people who, like me, were born into this industry. We were given a gift by our families, and we would not be able to do what we do if it weren't for them. We have a responsibility to take what we've learned and carry on the legacy. Working for Biale was never something that was forced upon me, it was always my decision to make. In fact, my dad encouraged me to become a lawyer. I am still uncertain of where my journey in the wine industry will take me, but I am proud to carry on their success and form my own identity at the same time.

It is such an exciting time to be living and working in the Napa Valley. California's wine industry is full of humble and talented people. I'm thankful to have such passionate peers. My dad once told me "Mags, wine and its myriad components add to our quality of life—like a gift we give to ourselves. We get to share its joy with others, and that's why our jobs are great." I don't think anyone can disagree with that. 🍷🍷

Establishing New Vines

Envolve Winery *BEN FLAJNIK, MIKE BENZIGER, DANNY FAY*

BNA Wine Group *TONY LEONARDINI*

Free Flow Wines *JORDAN KIVELSTADT*

Envolve Winery

BEN FLAJNIK, MIKE BENZIGER, DANNY FAY

Ben Flajnik, Danny Fay and Mike Benziger are fun-loving best friends and adventurous entrepreneurs determined to see their start-up thrive. Their credo is about approachability and community, all centered on Sonoma and biodynamic wines. They each bring unique experiences and expertise to the table, and the resulting dynamic mix of media and entrepreneurial capital positions Envolve for unprecedented success.

Long before wine became part of their lives, Ben, Danny and Mike were friends. They grew up playing baseball together in Sonoma, and they've returned to share Sonoma's pastime—wine.

One night in 2008, Ben and Mike were drinking crisp Sauvignon Blanc on the roof of their San Francisco apartment, baring their frustrations about working for other people. Immersed in different sectors of the wine industry, they had often talked about starting a wine business together. By the end of the bottle, they decided they would.

Their first move was to pool their resources. The Benziger family was willing to train Mike and Ben in its winemaking practices,

and the family's sterling reputation as a pioneer in the wine industry was a bonus. Meanwhile, Ben was a serial entrepreneur with a penchant for winemaking, ready to re-invest his earnings. As they ramped up, they asked Danny Fay, a trusted friend from Sonoma with a wine MBA from the Bordeaux Management School in France, to join as a partner in 2011. The three have been working together full-time for only two years, but production has already expanded from 350 to 20,000 cases.

"There are still days I think to myself, 'Why did I get into this business?' It's so frustrating! But, I love it. I *love* it," says Ben.

Envolve is growing so fast that the partners are pouring their

profits back into the company to make more wine and new labels. "It's amazing the wheels haven't come off yet," says Danny. When the company's ascent starts to flatten out, they want to move into their own facility customized to accommodate their annual production.

Message in a Bottle

Envolve Winery owns two labels: Envolve and Epilogue. They are both sourced from organic vineyards in Sonoma, but represent two tiers of pricing and craftsmanship. Envolve is more refined; Epilogue is a simple pleasure, like hearing a favorite song.

The Envolve labels are made with the winery's best grapes. Ranging from twenty dollars to forty dollars, the portfolio includes Sauvignon Blanc, Chardonnay, Rosé, Pinot Noir, Cabernet Sauvignon, Primitivo, a red Bordeaux blend and a sparkling wine.

Ben calls Epilogue his "Tuesday night wine," ranging between ten and sixteen dollars a bottle. Thus far, Epilogue's Chardonnay, Sauvignon Blanc and red Bordeaux blend are increasing sales monthly and sold in almost every state in the United States.

"Every bottle tells a story. Every vintage is a chapter. And, at the end of the wine's journey, you have its epilogue. That's the bottle itself," says Danny.

BEN F.

In 2011, Ben Flajnik (aka "Ben F.") was a contestant on ABC reality television show *The Bachelorette*, where he was one of Ashley Hebert's final two suitors. In 2012, he sought love again as featured bachelor on ABCs sister show, *The Bachelor*.

"The tangible rewards of this industry are amazing. You get to see people open a bottle, smile, and say, 'That's nice wine.'"

Their brands' appeal has been leveraged by Ben's involvement in the reality television show *The Bachelor*. The residual effects of Ben's pop culture presence has generated significant sales increases, particularly for Envolve's new sparkling wine label. It launched in September 2012, and might be their biggest hit yet. Bachelor and bachelorette parties have been renting out Envolve's tasting room since its inception, and now revelers fill flutes of Envolve's elegant sparkling wine during their celebrations. Though it was a good portfolio addition, Ben had to pay for the sparkling wine production with his personal American Express card, an expense that will be on his bill for some time.

Ben Flajnik

Ben has always loved the booze business, and he intends to master the art of fermentation. Ben and Mike, who were fast friends at an early age, experienced the underpinnings of the wine world as youngsters. In seventh grade, Ben started working with Mike at Benziger Family Winery in Sonoma, taking out the trash and doing other odd jobs around the property.

Ben's college experiences at the University of Arizona play into his career today. Ben majored in music production, and his ear for lyricism has brought a melodious sound to Envolve's label names. When he wasn't in class or playing soccer, he was working as an assistant brewer at Nimbus Brewery. Amid the stouts, pale ales and IPAs, Ben was introduced to yeast fermentation. He applied the concept to wine and made a Stags Leap AVA Merlot

and a Burgundian-style Chardonnay with purchased juice. As Ben completed the fermentation and aging process, his potential as a winemaker surfaced.

To continue his education, he and a friend started making a small wine label bottled in blue glass called Buona Spremuta, "good juice" in Italian. Between the free kegs at work and the artisan homemade wine, he always had something to pour at a party.

Though he's known for his mellowed-out personality, Ben's a man with vision and a carpe diem attitude. Born in 1982, he just turned thirty, and Envolve is his sixth startup. After college and a stint with an Internet advertising company, Ben started his own similar advertising firm. The timing was right and the industry was lucrative. By age twenty-three, he was a millionaire. He parlayed investments into a variety of startups ranging from a sunglasses company to an angel funding company. Then his dad, whom he was close to, passed away.

Devastated, Ben spent money as a way to deal with his dad's passing. He had two homes and countless cars. He coasted by without learning lessons. After a few years of reckless spending, Ben realized he was much happier before he made his quick money. In 2007, Ben made the choice to change his lifestyle and move back to northern California.

When Ben and Mike bottled their first Cabernet Sauvignon under the label Evolve (which they changed to Envolve in 2012),

they both had day jobs; Mike at Benziger Family Winery and Ben with his startups. Driven, they made time to work in wine bars and immerse themselves in the industry. They met and worked alongside Jordan Kivelstadt (profiled later in this book) at a wine bar and learned that he was also starting his own wine brands. A firestorm of creativity erupted between the three of them.

"Ahh, the summer of 2009," Ben says, reminiscing. "It was a great little 'think tank' for us wine geeks who were interested in sharing wine knowledge."

As Ben continued to build Envolve with Mike, it felt different from his other businesses. For the first time, Ben was starting to build a career in an industry he cared about.

"The tangible rewards of this industry are amazing. You get to see people open a bottle, smile, and say, 'That's nice wine.' Then, you give yourself a pat on the back, and think, 'I've just brightened someone's day.'"

When Ben started putting money behind Envolve, he was invited to join ABC's reality romance television show, *The Bachelorette*, and flew to Los Angeles to meet the bachelorette, Ashley Hebert. Julia Flajnik, Ben's sister, had submitted his name. After dates in Thailand, Taiwan and Fiji, Ben was one of the final two contestants vying for Ashley's hand in marriage. He proposed, but was rejected.

In this humbling experience, Ben found catharsis. He used the camera as a confessional. It was the first time he stopped to work through the emotions stemming from his father's death. *The Bachelorette* turned into a three-month intervention, an isolated time for self-reflection.

"It takes a while to find yourself," says Ben. "After *The Bachelorette*, I became a better son, a better brother and better friend."

As a side effect, the show helped Envolve gain recognition. Danny was called in to help out as sales skyrocketed. "We were just trying to get through each hour," says Mike. Almost immediately after settling back into a routine, Ben was asked to be the feature bachelor on ABC's reality show, *The Bachelor*. He and Mike had already set up their 2011 winemaking plan, so he didn't see any harm in accepting. To the benefit of Envolve and other local vintners, many episodes were shot in Sonoma. The TV series put Envolve on the map and changed Ben in ways he didn't expect. He was the center of the show and had to be decisive despite the scrutiny by his suitors and national media. He says the show was the hardest experience of his life; the controversies he endured were a far cry from the easy pace of farm-town Sonoma.

The Bachelor still has its effect on the brand's popularity and on Ben's personal life. He's the first winemaker to gain national exposure in popular culture through television. His challenge is to continue the momentum while building a reputation based on his love of wine, not romance.

Danny Fay

Danny was born in Oxford and spent his youth in Ducklington, a remote village in England where ducks still outnumber people. There weren't any fancy classes about wine in Ducklington. He'd never heard of grocery stores stocked with endless options for food or wine; there was just one convenience store that stocked his favorite breakfast, shredded wheat, and a milkman who delivered milk daily.

When Danny was ten, his dad Eamonn became restless in the rainy weather and sought out a new audio engineering job in sunny Palo Alto. After six months of reconnaissance, Eamonn moved the family to California. Although this move happened twenty years ago, Danny became a U.S. citizen in 2012—and passed the exam while flaunting American flag–printed sweatpants. Danny's early countrified days were grounding, and his

cumulative experiences have stimulated his worldly perspective.

Danny has always chosen the most challenging path to his goals. He doesn't shy away from obstacles, which harks back to his early days in Sonoma when he learned to socialize with his American peers. It wasn't easy being a British transfer student among middle school cliques, just as leading a new wine company among well-established wineries has its tricky moments.

After attending California Polytechnic State University in San Luis Obispo (and switching majors from aeronautical engineering to viticulture), Danny joined an international masters program for wine based in Bordeaux.

While Ben was traveling internationally on ABC's dime to take women out on dates, Danny was globe-trotting on behalf of his wine MBA program. Classes were held in several countries, including France, England, Australia and the United States. The eighteen-student program was geared toward older professionals, so its irregular schedule allowed Danny time to dip into entrepreneurial partnerships and unpredictable international adventures.

Danny's thesis on biodynamic viticulture was the result of his intensive study of organic and biodynamic vineyards in Argentina, Australia, Austria, California, France, New Zealand, Oregon and Spain. Biodynamics started in 1924 from a series of lectures in Germany, which relayed nine ideal steps to enhance soil fertilization. True biodynamic farmers use the lunar calendar to plant, bury cow horns filled with manure in the ground, spray crushed quartz mixtures on the vines and till herbs into the soil.

■

DOG DAYS

Ben's Jack Russell terrier, Scotch, is the brand's mascot. He travels everywhere
with the boys, and can often be found digging for gophers on vineyard grounds.

"It is the right thing to do for the land. It builds the vitality of
the natural soil, producing a healthier vineyard for the future,
whereas conventional farming diminishes it," says Mike.

Danny had a number of influences, from Pete Hoffman and Mark Burningham of Benziger Family Winery to Peter Proctor, author of *One Man, One Cow, One Planet*. Proctor, who calculates that modern agriculture erodes topsoil at three million tons per hour, sees biodynamics as an environmental necessity. Danny attended Proctor's lectures and made compost teas with Hoffman to understand and eventually appreciate the philosophical elements and theory behind biodynamics.

After finals, Danny headed to the Greek Isles and Cyprus for a breather. He was at a bar in Cyprus when Mike called. Ben had made it pretty far in *The Bachelorette*, and the popularity of their wine brand was growing. Mike was still working for his family while "slinging Envolve wines out the back door." They needed help from someone they could trust. Danny was swayed by the mutual interest in biodynamics, and he joined Envolve in June 2011 with an equity position and CEO responsibilities.

Danny's responsible for Envolve's marketing, branding, finance and employee management, while Mike and Ben share responsibilities as chief operating officers. When Mike or Ben come up with creative ideas, Danny finds a way to actualize the plan. He's constantly forecasting and strategizing. Now that the team has people in place to do time-consuming tasks like accounting and filing, Danny can focus on creating a balanced and profitable company.

"Every day you're challenging yourself to beat the competition, to sell your wine, and to get into the mindset of the consumer," says Danny.

Shaping Envolve's Identity

During Envolve's earlier startup stages, Ben, Danny and Mike lived together in a two bedroom apartment in San Francisco. Danny relived the nomadic lifestyle of his MBA program and slept on a mattress in the living room. They ate, worked late nights, traveled and socialized together. It resulted in synchronized business values and a cohesive mission to bring Sonoma out of Napa's shadow with quality wines and constant outreach.

There's one obvious way to sell wine that the partners refuse to take: putting Ben's face on the bottle or calling it "Bachelor Ben's Bacchanal." But to appease fans while remaining true to Envolve's principles, the partners keep a stash of Ben Flajnik-signed bottles at their warehouse. They're proud to be "normal" winemakers and will grow their business organically.

"People put two and two together; they aren't stupid. So, yes, we get more sales because of *The Bachelor*. But, for example, we approached distributors on the east coast who didn't know about the show. They were fifty-five-year-old men in smoking jackets, but they put our brand in seven states because they liked our wine and our price point," recounts Danny.

Danny considers Ben's fame a double-edged sword. He estimates that 30 to 40 million people, roughly 10 percent of the U.S. population, recognize Ben as "Bachelor Ben." It's Danny's challenge to steer people to the wine-oriented side of Ben and re-identify him as "Winemaker Ben."

When Mike isn't feet deep in grapes, he's watching the New York Giants. Almost every Sunday during football season, Mike paints his face, wears a Giants jersey and roots on his favorite team.

"There is this gray area between Envolve's brand reach and *The Bachelor*'s brand reach. In that gray area is where people make presumptions about our product," he says. "People might question our authenticity, wine quality, or sustainability, but the reality is that we've worked very hard to create something much greater than ourselves in a very cool, fun industry."

Mike Benziger

Ben and Danny both agree that the business wouldn't have had a chance without the help of the Benzigers. Mike has been an integral part of his family's wine business since he could walk. When Mike was four years old, his Uncle Mike, now Sonoma's patriarch of biodynamic farming, asked his parents, Bruno and Helen, and his six siblings to transplant from New York and form a family winery. He was persuasive, and the whole family packed up and moved west.

"When they came here, it was the wild west of the industry. The first year, my uncles made wine in the back of a milk truck because our tanks weren't delivered before harvest," says Mike. The milk truck wine won awards, and soon after, marketing-master Bruno turned the family name into a big business. Benziger's low-cost, Sonoma-based brand, Glen Ellen, grossed 135 million dollars annually and became the ninth best-selling label in the country in 1992. Around the same time, the Benzigers sold Glen Ellen and launched Benziger Family Winery as a high-end brand. With about two dozen family members involved, Benziger is still one of the most influential family businesses in Sonoma.

In 1993, the Benzigers were exploring new ways to develop premium wines. They were intrigued by the concept of organic farming, but didn't investigate it until a wine consultant named Alan York personally presented a case for biodynamic farming— a step beyond organic farming. The family sought out a real-life example, and after a trip to Fetzer Vineyards in Mendocino,

California, they were sold. Shortly after, the Benzigers implemented biodynamic farming on their home estate and were smitten with the resulting wines. This property is their source for their premium Bordeaux blend, Tribute, the first biodynamic wine from either Sonoma or Napa County.

"The wines that come from our properties have certain flavors and nuances that can only come from that property and can only be extracted by biodynamic farming," says Mike proudly.

Now the Benzigers open their home estate as a show property for biodynamic farming, and students from around the world come to learn. Mike was privileged with an insider's view of biodynamic wine production. He knew he would be welcomed into the family business if he decided to join after college, but he wasn't pressured.

"My family has been so supportive. They told me, 'You can do whatever you want. If you want to run a coffee stand, we'll get you going and give you the business training,'" he says.

Mike may have considered such a career—or, really, anything but wine. After spending the majority of his formative years working for the family business, he distanced himself from the industry and his family by moving to New York for college. At Manhattanville College, he focused on basketball and refused to talk about wine. After graduation, dinner parties became an active part of his social life, and he reconnected with the memorable dining experiences and lasting friendships of his younger years. Nostalgia for Sonoma and Benziger Family Winery kicked in. He missed the unique geography of his hometown; there weren't any vineyards or rolling hills in Manhattan. So Mike moved to San Francisco and worked in Benziger's tasting room and on the winemaking team. In between various roles at the winery, he worked in sales for a California wine distributor, an experience that prepared him well for the sales trips he now makes with Ben.

Through Envolve, Mike understands exactly what his family went through in its early days of entrepreneurship. When he's not making wine, he's selling it. In a three-week span, Mike and Ben typically visit five or six states. There's a lot of dining, wine tasting, lugging bottles around and playing golf with representatives from distribution companies. It sounds like a life of luxury, but Mike and Ben are constantly educating and promoting their wine while getting a feel for the market. Each day is packed with tasting events, bottle signings and press interviews.

"The hours definitely pile up. They can be long and grueling, but we keep plugging away," he says resolutely.

Sauvignon Blanc Winemaking

Envolve is a "Sauvignon Blanc house," since this was the variety that launched the label. Sauvignon Blanc is their golden goose businesswise too. Unoaked white wines demand a lower capital investment, because they can be bottled and sent to market about six months after harvest. It's called "tank to bank". In contrast, the Cabernet Sauvignon grapes harvested in 2012 won't be released in bottle until 2016. Envolve hedges a four-year bet on Cabernet Sauvignon, paying for the grapes and barrels up front.

Envolve sources its fruit from biodynamically farmed vineyards. The partners favor biodynamic fruit quality and believe it's the most natural way of farming. They like that it's focused on self-contained ecosystems designed to keep the good bugs in and the bad bugs and diseases out.

"It is the right thing to do for the land. It builds the vitality of the natural soil, producing a healthier vineyard for the future, whereas conventional farming diminishes it," says Mike.

Mike and Ben learned about biodynamic farming together when they worked for Mike's uncles, and Danny learned the same methods from the Benzigers while preparing for his thesis. Their common experience made it easy for them to decide to produce biodynamic wines. Ben, Mike and Danny have all been persuaded by Mike's family's farming approach, but their similarities reverberate beyond biodynamics. "Each of the family members in my dad's generation has had a different role in influencing the company," says Mike.

On sales trips, distributors often share stories of their encounters with Mike's grandfather, Bruno. Bruno's legacy has opened as many doors among distributors as *The Bachelor* has among consumers. Mike and Ben's mentors, Joe Benziger and Mark Burningham, vice president of winegrowing at Benziger Family Winery, have helped them sculpt their ideal flavor profile for each variety. Mike and Ben have gained confidence as winemakers, but they still reach out to their mentors for second opinions.

The partners are all finding their own individual mentors, too. Ben recently began studying with Dan Kosta, of Kosta Browne, who has openly shared his book of winemaking secrets. Danny has many mentors on the business side with whom he formed relationships during his MBA program. Mike still counts on the older generation of Benzigers for advice, and on his younger sister, Kate, too. She's a junior partner at Envolve, where she manages customer relations, inventory, and marketing. The dynamic of their sibling relationship has matured, and Mike fondly considers Kate the "nerve center" of Envolve's brand outreach.

Tasting Room

In 2012, Envolve opened a tasting room off the main square in the town of Sonoma. This is the partners' public statement that they're in it for the long haul.

Opening weekend festivities set the tone for the company's

Ben's father passed in 2006, and he laces up his father's leather shoes every harvest to keep memories of him close to heart.

branding direction. Ben in high cotton socks with shorts and a worn gray T-shirt sat on the granite patio steps, swaying along to his musically talented friends' songs while refilling the flutes of those sitting next to him. Mike was giving an encouraging word to the employees behind the bar, while Danny was surrounded by a group of wine club members eating delivery pizza and pouring several just-purchased Envolve wines. *Mi casa es su casa.* The space, equipped with wide-screen televisions, board games, a chalkboard full of customer comments ("speed date night, please!") and indoor and outdoor seating, has been received with open arms by neighboring tasting rooms; however, Ben, Danny and Mike are careful not to step on any toes.

"A great theme park doesn't have just one great roller coaster. It takes many attractions to create a destination," says Danny.

Despite a doubling of Envolve's staff since opening last summer, all hands are still on deck. When Ben, Danny and Mike are in their Sonoma office at the same time, they're often talking on the phone while responding to e-mails. As Ben reads a customer e-mail out loud, Danny pauses from his phone call with a local sign maker to listen. Mike, listening too, sits at a table piled high with government liquor approvals and types an email on his cell phone. He sends a few more e-mails, then asks Danny and Ben if they want to come over after work to grill some steaks and watch the San Francisco Giants, their favorite baseball team. They laugh about something Danny says, and for a brief moment they're a bunch of friends joking around. Then the banter halts as Ben answers a phone call from a representative at Whole Foods Market. With a quick high-five to Mike and Danny, he leaves the room and gets down to business.

"I'm legal, accounting, sales, winemaking, production, and compliance. We all do so many different jobs. It's a bit ridiculous, but it's what we have to do," says Ben with a grin. ▮▮

Envolve Winery

Winemakers: Mike Benziger, Ben Flajnik

SONOMA, CA

Established 2008

Known for its Sauvignon Blanc and Pinot Noir

Focused on biodynamic wines

Partners Mike Benziger, Ben Flajnik and Danny Fay are best friends and grew up in Sonoma

Ben Flajnik honored with a proclamation by Sonoma's mayor, Joanne Sanders for *The Bachelor's* positive portrayals of Sonoma, increasing tourism and sales tax by proxy

EnvolveWinery.com

Two months after grape buds break through the vines, they cluster and flower. Flowering signifies a period of pollination and fertilization, resulting in a grape berry.

BNA Wine Group

TONY LEONARDINI

Tony Leonardini's alter ego as a volunteer firefighter is as unexpected as Peter Parker's Spider Man, but Tony has more in common with the comic book hero than the guy next door. By profession, Tony's a winemaker, but at every opportunity, he suits up and fights fire. His eyes are constantly roving for action, whether it's a fire truck on the move or an old pickup truck racing by his vineyards. Confident as a Nantucket yachtsman, Tony is just as comfortable in water as on land. Almost every morning, Tony can be spotted swimming in the numbing San Francisco Bay, training to swim the English Channel.

volunteer

NAPA VALLEY
CABERNET SAUVIGNON

NAPA VALLEY
CABERNET SAUVIGNON

Despite Tony's wholesome charisma, he's never been a crowd-pleaser. From a young age, he wouldn't kowtow to the whims of the popular kids. In middle school, Tony was bullied and made fun of as the "wine kid", because his parents owned a wine cellar, a wine shop and a winery. This was the early 1980s when Napa's wine industry was still largely blue-collared and under-developed. Throughout high school, he never talked about his family because of all the abuse he received from his peers. But as those same kids grew up and turned into wine drinkers, they recalled Tony's wine connection and wanted to make amends.

A Perfect Pairing

When Tony wasn't at school, he was surrounded by the wine business, and his learning compounded. At age five, Tony worked at his father's wine shop, breaking down cardboard boxes for a nickel each. His dad quizzed him about different wine varietals over dinner like a teacher quizzing a student about state capitals. When his parents bought Whitehall Vineyards in Napa, Tony's education accelerated. He worked in Whitehall's tasting room and made barrels of Cabernet on the side—barrels he took with

him when he decided to separate emotionally and physically from the family business and find his own identity.

In 2006, Tony set out on his own. He valeted and catered to afford time for his hobbies of making wine and volunteering as a fireman at the local station. Tony understood that if he wanted to make another vintage of wine, he needed to brand and sell his Cabernet. Then one afternoon after putting out a fire, he thought of a name: Volunteer.

Almost immediately after bottling Volunteer, Tony got a call from a friend-of-a-friend who worked for a distributor called "Triple C," in Knoxville, Tennessee, asking for a pallet—672 bottles of Volunteer. Two weeks later, the man called asking for another pallet. It didn't seem real. Tony asked the manager of Triple C how he was selling the wine so fast.

The answer was simple: Tennessee is the "Volunteer State."

Within four years, Tony built a one-man business with three labels: Volunteer, Bandwagon and Rule. It became Little Lion Wine Company, a translation of his last name *leonardini*, meaning "little lion." In 2009, Tony partnered with two seasoned Tennessee men, and they launched BNA Wine Group to bring national exposure to Tony's wines. To reinforce the brand's southern roots, they adopted Nashville's BNA airport code.

Tennessee has been pivotal in Tony's career. As the only Napa wine company with headquarters in Nashville, BNA maintains an element of distinction. His two other founding partners, John Hooper, a fourth generation wine and spirits distributor, and sales veteran Gary Carr, are highly respected in the wine and spirits distribution industry. Almost all of BNA's wines are still sourced in Napa, and Tony retains a satellite office in St. Helena. With the founders' trifecta of talent, they intend to sell 100,000 cases (1.2 million bottles) of wine this year.

Within weeks, they both called. "We need more Butternut."

TESTING A GRAPE'S CHARACTER

Tony Leonardini employs innovative methods of testing and monitoring his grapes. He sends grapes to science labs in Napa to test their sugar levels.

"We want the best grapes," said Tony. "Why would we let an imaginary line between California and Oregon stop us?"

Experimenting with Technology

Tony's business partners are banking on his potential as a wine-maker, but he doesn't seem to feel the pressure. His immunity to stress allows breathing room for creativity and experiments, and his individualistic character helps him rise above petty outside influences and "rules." Because of this, Tony says no one is making wine like BNA.

Tony is always eager to experiment with more precise ways to ferment, bottle and sell grapes. He's unafraid to ask questions or test his own methods. Two years ago, Tony started playing around with GoPros—small attachable waterproof and shock-proof video cameras used commonly for adventure photography —to assess his wine. At one point after harvest, he thought something was wrong with the uptake of the grape's residual yeast, called "lees," which is stirred to add flavor complexity to Chardonnay. He stuck his GoPro into the vat, let it record for a while, then took it out and replayed the video. Tony was right: the yeast deposits were clumped and not where they should have been.

To solve the problem, Tony bought a custom fermentation mixer, similar to a KitchenAid, but forty times the size. It was the only "mixer" used at a winery in the United States, and decades old at that. He let it run twenty-four hours a day for two months, compared the results to his vats, and decided the mixers made better wine. Tony is applying this experiment to different lots each year, and slowly intends to use the mixer for all of his grapes.

Tony's enthusiasm for invention seems endless. Recently, he had a cooperage in France create a wine barrel with one French oak head and one American oak head, and staves alternating between American and French oak. Several times during the grape-growing season, Tony picks 100 grapes from one row and 100 grapes from another row, and sends them to a lab. The lab's enologists report the grapes' sugar levels and other components, which helps Tony determine the flavor profile and readiness of each vineyard.

Of BNA's current portfolio, Tony says that his biggest feat is Butternut. In 2009, Tony fermented wine from Chardonnay grapes that overoxidized, a result of too much volatile acidity, making them smell like nail polish. The grapes were super ripe and sat on the lees for a long time. Despite what Tony calls "grammatical mistakes," the juice tasted surprisingly good. Though other winemakers might have justified dumping the juice, Tony knew he couldn't just throw away his investment. He had to decide what to do.

While watching TV and reading one night, Tony noticed his wife, Melissa, walk in with a veggie box from the local farmer's market. The butternut squash caught his eye. "Butternut, that's a great name," Tony thought to himself. After a quick search online to see if anyone had taken the name, Tony found that it was available. He called his now-partner John Hooper to offer him the wine. John loved the name and said he'd take it all.

From web traffic analysis, Tony knew his primary customers were 25 to 35 year-old women, so he asked a young woman in Colorado to design a label that would appeal to her. Within weeks of the wine's release, John called. "We need more Butternut."

Butternut is still a best seller for BNA, and it's still an over-the-top Chardonnay.

French Connection

At home, Tony doesn't talk much shop. His time is devoted to his two-year-old daughter, Eva, and wife Melissa. Eva tends to fall and bruise herself often and is curious about everything she can touch and taste. When Tony and Melissa aren't preoccupied with her, they muse over flippant celebrity news and other less-than-serious topics. Until Eva's birth, Melissa spent her working life in the wine business, so she understands Tony almost intuitively.

Tony's brother-in-law, Dave Phinney, is his closest mentor. Dave is best known for his wine The Prisoner, the label with Goya's "Le Petit Prisonnier" painting and scratchy 1600s pirate typography. Prisoner is a swash of Zinfandel and Cabernet grapes culled from the leftovers of various high-end vineyards. Dave built and owns a winery in Maury, France, making wine with French grapes in a California style. Tony and Melissa drink a lot of Dave's wine—quite the perk—and Tony keeps a few spare bottles of Dave's Zinfandel label, Saldo, in the office.

It was Dave who told Tony to keep his bottle prices low, so the wine would exceed customers' expectations. This advice was unusual; many of Tony's peers were taking advantage of the Napa name to inflate prices. When Tony was debating whether to use screw-top bottle closures, he called up Dave, who asked a simple question: "Do you like screw tops?" Tony didn't. Today, he still uses corks.

In the industry, Tony believes that the later part of this decade will be a real test for Napa. To counter some of Napa's vineyard real estate issues, Tony has decided to experiment, again, and mix Pinot Noir grapes from Oregon and California to make his 2011 Bandwagon label. Tony won't be able to say the wine is from California, but he's an unconfined man, indifferent to tradition.

"We want the best grapes," says Tony. "Why would we let an imaginary line between California and Oregon stop us?" ❢❢

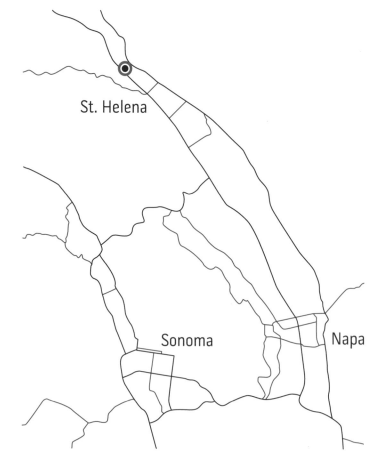

BNA Wine Group
Winemaker: Tony Leonardini
ST. HELENA, CA

....

Established 2010

Known for its The Rule, Bandwagon, Butternut and Volunteer wines

BNA will sell 1.2 million bottles of wine this year

The wines are made in Napa, but the business is headquartered in Nashville, TN

BNA is the airport code for Nashville, TN

Tony is a volunteer firefighter

....

BNAwinegroup.com

Free Flow Wines

JORDAN KIVELSTADT

With two entrepreneurial parents, Jordan Kivelstadt was destined to start his own venture. Or two. Or three. Jordan is CEO of Free Flow Wines, the premier wine-kegging business in the United States, and is also owner and winemaker of Qualia Wines, an artisanal Sonoma wine brand. Jordan forges ahead of competitors with one goal in mind: he's going to change the way America drinks wine.

Free Flow focuses on product quality and environmental impact. Its system significantly reduces the industry's carbon footprint while preserving the wine and reducing spoilage. One keg eliminates 26 wine bottles along with their corks, labels, foils and cardboard shipping boxes.

with wine from stainless steel tanks. Each tank is sent from a particular winery, with instructions from the winemaking team to tweak the wine before it's kegged, so it tastes just right. Once the kegs are full, they move into the fulfillment center where they're tagged and then shipped. A special mobile software system provides Free Flow and its clients with up-to-date tracking. Every keg has an adhesive sticker with a "Born On" date, a color identifying whether the wine is red or white and a stamp with a unique 2D barcode.

Wine on tap is becoming popular in Los Angeles, San Francisco, Sonoma, Napa, Atlanta and Grand Traverse Bay, Michigan. Informal restaurants like California Pizza Kitchen and hotels like Marriott International and Starwood Hotels and Resorts Worldwide are especially embracing it. Jordan frequently travels to meet with national corporations to systemize their wine-on-tap programs. Free Flow's kegs keep wine fresh for six weeks from the day they're first tapped. What's more, proprietors reduce their recycling fees in states that mandate bottle disposal. By partnering with Free Flow, Caesars Palace in Las Vegas saves four tons of trash annually.

Despite Free Flow's success, Jordan and Dan are constantly dispelling myths about kegs. There are companies across the country that aren't as quality-conscious as Free Flow. Nothing kills an industry or an idea faster than having a bad product in the market, says Jordan. While Free Flow is quickly proving the viability of premium wines on-tap. It's now endorsed by Master Sommeliers like Bobby Stuckey, Emily Wines and Rob Bigelow.

Free Flow is on tap at award-winning restaurants owned by star chefs like Gordon Ramsay and Daniel Boulud.

Installing wine-on-tap systems can be costly, so restaurants with wine taps are betting on a long-term return. Typically, restaurants save five percent on the cost of wine. While kegs continue to take hold, there are still a few kinks. Free Flow is a young company addressing decades-old problems. There are three predominant issues with wine-on-tap: setup, service and temperature. If any of these are off-kilter, the wine can spoil or taste flat.

"Wine-on-tap is a new category and is not without its learnings," says Jordan. "As we work with our clients, we teach them its nuances."

In the setup process, many establishments use plastic tubing from the keg to the tapping spigot, which oxygenates wine and tires it out quickly. To solve this problem, Jordan helped create a wine-only tubing that's 100 times more oxygen resistant than any beer line.

Once the kegs are set up, the temperature of the wine can cause problems, although bottled wine, as Jordan diplomatically points out, faces temperature issues, too. To ensure the white wines aren't too warm and the reds wines aren't too cool, Free Flow worked with Micro Matic to introduce a dual-zone kegerator. It's based on thirty prototypes that Jordan hand-built, and it ensures that the wine is always served at the right temperature.

Qualia is a Latin philosophy term which refers to an individual's sensory experiences in the world and its ultimate influence on human perspective.

A Blend of Business and Boutique Wine

For about half an hour every day, Jordan becomes "winemaker" of Qualia instead of "CEO" of Free Flow. Qualia started as an extension of his Pavo label, but it has become its own entity. Depending on the day, Jordan might be sampling wine from his monogrammed "JCK" barrels or streamlining Free Flow's inventory orders on Excel. Jordan is much better known for Free Flow, but he derives just as much pleasure from Qualia.

The Qualia winery is conveniently located at the front of Free Flow's warehouse. Several friends in the business make wine there as well. During harvest, Jordan comes into the winery with a T-shirt on, works on his wines, then changes into a polo shirt and walks to the back of the warehouse where he resumes CEO duties. The Qualia portfolio includes a Syrah, a Syrah–Grenache blend, a Carignan, a Sauvignon Blanc, and a Carignan–Mourvèdre rosé blend. Jordan loves teaching his customers about wine, especially about lesser-known varieties like Carignan and Mourvèdre. The grapes come from vineyards in Sonoma County, located about an hour and a half north of the Golden Gate Bridge.

"Consumers have absolutely no idea what they're getting when they buy Syrah. There are so many different styles. I'd like to get together with other Syrah winemakers and find a way to explain and define the variety to drinkers," says Jordan.

With the exception of the harvest season, Jordan only has time to spend about three hours a week on Qualia. So he leaves the day-to-day responsibilities to his employee, twenty-five year old Alex Pomerantz. Alex sees himself as an understudy with the responsibility to fulfill Jordan's vision for the brand.

Ten years from now, Jordan would like to devote himself to Qualia while sitting on the board of Free Flow. He has a soft spot for artisanal winemaking. "Qualia is a lifelong passion project," he says. 🍷🍷

Free Flow Wines
CEO: Jordan Kivelstadt
SONOMA, CA

Established 2009

Free Flow manages and distributes premium wine in kegs

Removed 660,000 bottles, corks and labels last year via wine-on-tap

Free Flow's custom engineered kegs eliminate the possibility of cork taint, reducing wine spoilage

Jordan is also winemaker and owner of Qualia Wines, known for its Syrah

FreeFlowWines.com

Jordan Kivelstadt, Alex Pomerantz and Qualia's vineyard harvest crew working with tractor headlights and personal headlamps.

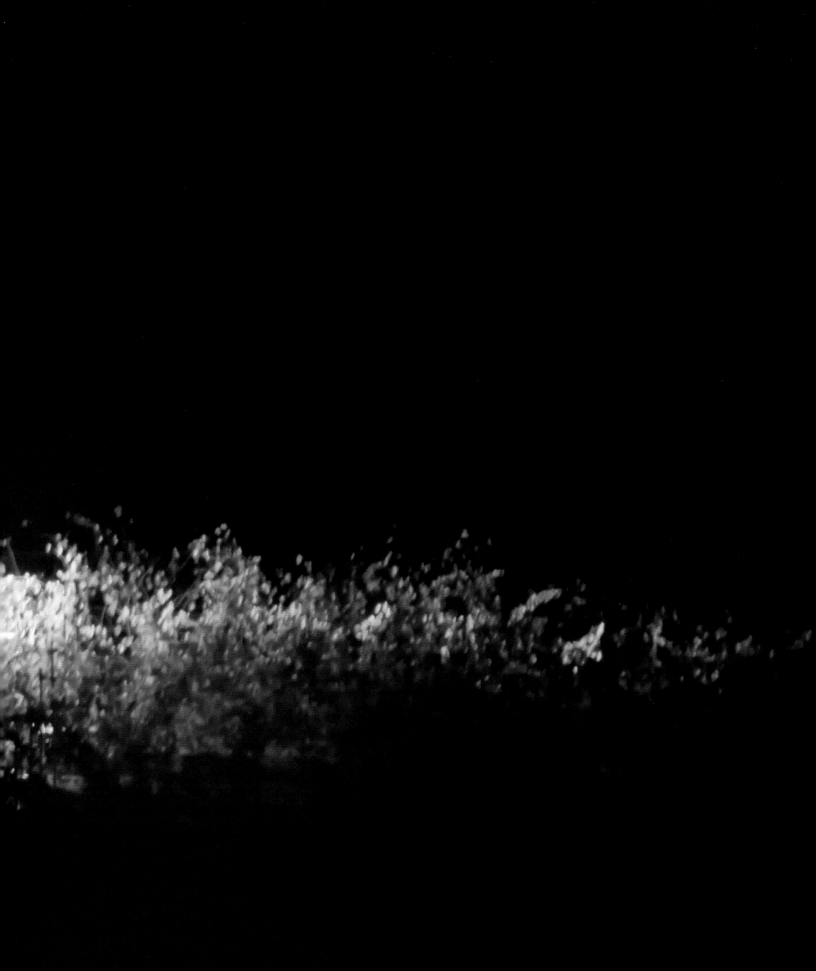

Cult to Classic

PAUL ROBERTS
Master Sommelier
Estate Director, Bond Estate
Oakville, California

Paul Roberts, MS is an oenophile with the meticulous habits and warm hospitality of a world-class sommelier. As current director of Bond Estates and the former corporate wine director for The Thomas Keller Restaurant Group, he has experienced the best of wine and cuisine. As the first Texan to become a Master Sommelier, and only the sixth person to pass on the first try, Paul brings a profound understanding of terroir to Bond Estates and its 'Grand Cru' quality wines.

In his discussion with author Chelsea Prince, Paul speaks to the history of the term "cult wine", California's winemaking culture and his opinion on serving premium wine on tap.

Q: What is your opinion on the term cult wine?

The term "cult wine" was originally coined by a writer in the 1990s to describe six wine brands which produced wines from very small properties that aimed to achieve the greatness of highly-ranked wines in Bordeaux. Harlan Estate is one of those original six. "Cult wine" is an easy to remember moniker, so its usage became widespread. We were happy to get the attention in Napa, but it became a saying that none of the wineries actually created.

In the early 1990s, there were several less-than-stellar vintages from Bordeaux. Meanwhile, Napa was experiencing a string of very excellent years. Understandably, people were really trying to grab up Bordeaux-style blends from these single-vineyard estates in Napa. It created a have-to-have-it, cult-like rush. The word cult signifies something that comes and goes, and I don't think any of us are trying to be a bright light that fades away. It's time for a new name. If you look at the Araujos or the Colgins, for example, it's obvious they're creating a long-term winegrowing vision. We are all trying to replace the word "cult" with "classic." Classic wines in Napa are going to last for a long time.

Q: How would you describe California wine country's wine making culture? Is it unique?

California is such a huge, diverse place. We produce two dollar wines and 2,000 dollar wines. We grow all of the major grapes you find in France. The winemaking may not be different, but the consumer is. The clamor for "newness" is something very different. It's amazing, and it's dangerous. Think about Manifest Destiny; the idea was to go West and do something different. We're excited by what's new: new cars, new movies, new wines. It's why I think the United States' wine market is the most exciting in the world. I think the best wine minds, like Aldo Sohm, are in the U.S. because we have such a dynamic consumer market. We have the privilege to see and taste wines from everywhere in the world.

At the same time, we often dismiss brands that aren't new. If a winery has been around for twenty-five years, it's most likely done something right. Sometimes we forget about the people that brought us to the dance.

Q: What is the importance of mentors?

I think mentorship is important in any business, maybe even more so in this industry. You need to learn what the wine does. You only get to harvest once a year and sometimes you have to rely on passed-down knowledge. You don't have to have a mentor to make great wines, but you can rise up the steep learning curve much faster. Morgan [Peterson], for example, (profiled in this book) has the best mentor—his dad.

Q: What is your opinion of premium wines served on tap?

I think it's terrific on so many fronts. As the former head Sommelier at The French Laundry, I would say it's a dream come true for restaurateurs to guarantee freshness and cut down on waste. I was at a restaurant recently that had about 10 wines on tap. I asked if I could have one ounce of all ten, I just wanted to try everything. And, I could. Because of this, I found some producers I've never heard of.

I don't think you can put every wine in a keg because it's not always the perfect vessel. But, it's an excellent delivery method for 90 percent of the wine brands out there. The wine industry as a whole needs to be doing more to get a 21-year-old to buy a five dollar glass of Cabernet instead of a five dollar beer. Premium kegged wines, if they are maintained properly, will broaden our reach.

Q: How does one decide when to open a bottle of Bond?

Aging wine has its benefits, but sometimes you need to pull the cork and open a bottle of something good. You never know what tomorrow could bring. I promise you, [Bond] will taste great tonight, and it will taste great in 10 years, so you make the decision.

Harvesting the
New Crop of Talent

Futo *JASON EXPOSTO*

Far Niente *NICOLE MARCHESI*

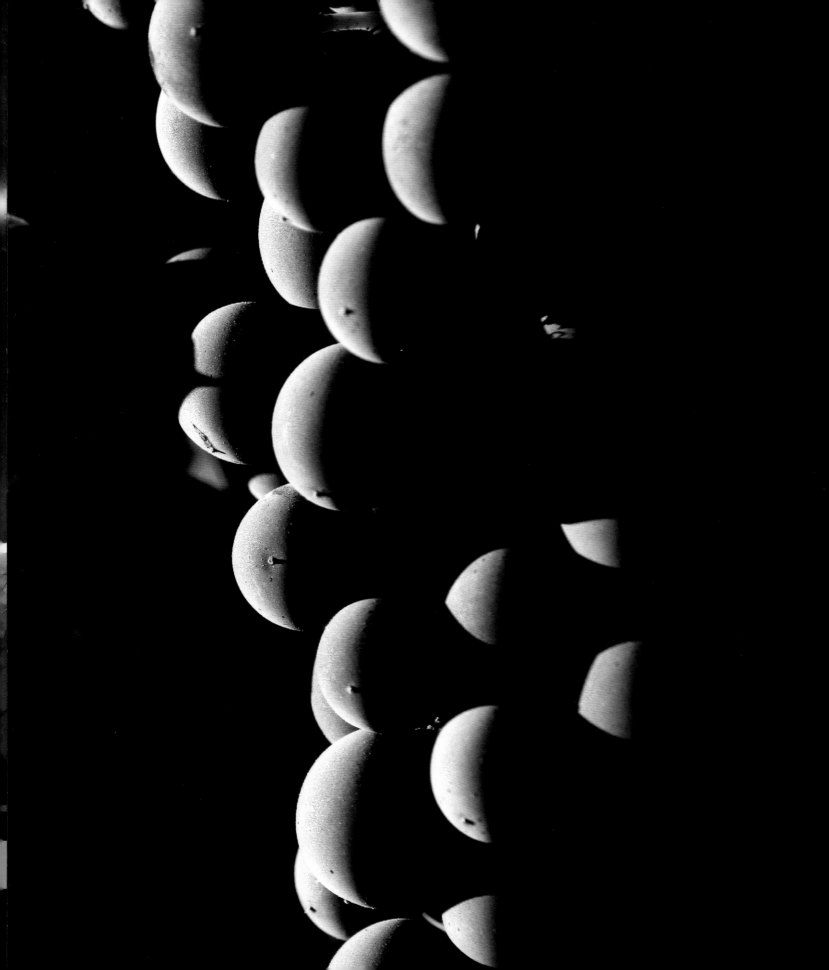

LAND OF PLENTY

The hillside property is particularly lush compared to the rest
of water-deprived Napa. Jason often finds hidden chanterelle
mushrooms on its grounds.

Jason works at one of Napa's most discreet wineries, hidden in the hills of Oakville. The Futo Estate has a custom-built winery constructed to reflect its character. When the rare visitor sees its dramatic fermentation room, Jason shrugs, smiles, and calls it a "fancy barn". Backlit magnum bottles spiral down a cement staircase, leading from the fermentation room to the barrel room, where the walls are lined with barrels. There isn't a dent or scratch anywhere, or even a creak. In its stillness, the winery resembles a shrine.

A husband-and-wife team, Tom and Kyle Futo from Kansas, developed the namesake winery in homage to their favorite California wines. They first developed an interest in international wines, then honed in on California. There was something irresistible about its wines, and they swooned over the wines made from winemaking consultants Helen Turley and Tony Soter. In 2002, Tom purchased the winery formerly known as Oakford Vineyards, adjacent to one of Napa's crown jewel wineries, Harlan Estate.

Like Futo, many small-scale wineries are taking chances on young, potentially knockout winemakers like Jason. What's happening now is an overlap between the generations, doubling the talent pool. Many trusted wine consultants haven't hit retirement and are still employed by some of the very same wineries. At Futo, Jason has the opportunity to shape its reputation from dirt to bottle. Jason is humble, reserved, enthusiastic and focused. His ever-present smile may be wide and serene, but he's a man to be taken seriously. Jason is intense about his work, and he watches over the property like a shepherd.

"I want to make an original wine. Absolutely original. I want someone to taste the wine and say, 'Oh, that's Futo.'"

The term cult wine too often pokes its head up like a gopher in a vineyard, and is used to categorize wineries like Futo. As Paul Roberts, estate director of another "cult" winery, says in Rock and Vine's Q&A, "The term 'cult wine' was originally coined by a writer in the 1990s to describe six wine brands which produced wines from very small properties that aimed to achieve the greatness of highly-ranked wines in Bordeaux." At the time, Bordeaux vintages were receiving poor reviews, so wine enthusiasts grabbed up California estate-made wines to fill the void. It has now been more than a decade since this California wine rush occurred, and many, including Jason and Paul, find the term archaic and meaningless. There's no classification for Futo's site-specific wine, other than its name, says Jason.

While Jason may believe he has nothing to do with the excellence of the wine, there's no doubt that he's an indispensable part of the equation. Jason is wise beyond his years in his land-before-hands approach, but his personal touch creates distinctive wines that can last for a lifetime.

Before "winemaker" ever crossed his mind, Jason wanted to be a chef or an architect. His dad, a chef, gave Jason little sips of Italian wine while cooking in the kitchen. At sixteen, Jason went to work at a winery lab. One day, the winemaker lined up forty glasses of the winery's wines and asked Jason what he thought about each one. Jason was intrigued when he tasted a difference in each wine. He kept asking, "Why?" "How?"

"I want to make an original wine. Absolutely original. I want someone to taste the wine and say, "Oh, that's Futo."

F U T O

From then on, Jason shirked homework and surrounded himself with wine. When he wasn't asking questions of anyone who'd answer, he was reading textbooks about viticulture and enology. By the end of his senior year in high school, he decided to study wine to figure it all out.

His excitement over vineyard details satisfied his scientific inclinations, while the art of winemaking satisfied his creativity. After graduation, Jason persuaded winemakers making the best international Bordeaux-varietals that he was going to work for them. With his easy demeanor and knack for winemaking, Jason always got the job. Now that Jason's making one of the most promising Cabernets in America, he grins when he thinks about how he used to peek over Futo's stone-wall hedge, eyeing the winery like a kid does his favorite candy.

In his transition from protégé to superstar, Jason's had the fine fortune to explore the different roads taken by winemakers from around the world. His former bosses, including the California iconoclast winemaker David Abreu of Abreu Vineyard, the Bordeaux consultant Stéphane Derenoncourt and the New Zealand winemaker Steve Smith MW of Craggy Range Winery,

most influence his winemaking style. Jason took detailed notes at each job, yet he realizes success boils down to hard work and the ability to intimately know Futo's complex site. Since his promotion to winemaker at Futo, Jason has relied on obsessing over vineyard and vintage details, as well as lessons from his mentors to inform his current decisions. Futo produces only 1,000 cases of each vintage, and like *Willy Wonka & The Chocolate Factory*, the gates stay closed to visitors.

Gentleness and preservation are the key words Jason uses to describe his winemaking. He focuses on capturing the singular characters of the site, which have "piercing purity combined with power, and complexity while retaining a weightless quality." During harvest, Futo's ten full-time vineyard workers begin handpicking grapes at 4 a.m., placing clusters into micro-bins that hold eight to ten pounds of fruit. Fruit is then sorted by hand. The grapes are placed on a complex series of conveyors where stems and imperfect grape clusters are removed, then crushed, before dropping by gravity into the fermentation tanks. After aging, the wine is also moved by gravity flow to the bottling line. Gravity-fed production is important to Futo's hands-off winemaking philosophy. Jason doesn't like to pump

Futo makes a second wine, "OV," short for Oakford Vineyards. The name is
a tribute to the land's history, and its former ownership.

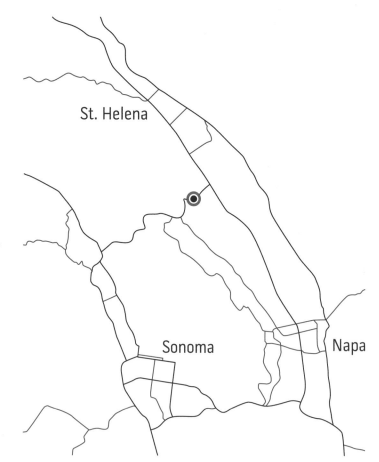

the wine because that changes its delicate aromas.

"The goal is for the bottled wine to capture the fullest essence of
the fruit just as it tastes at harvest," says Jason.

Natural Selection

Futo's home is in the rolling elevations of western Oakville. It
sits amid wild, old forests, and where chanterelle mushrooms
grow along the creeks. It's important to Jason that the land
remain biodiverse and that the disruption to natural vegetation
is minimal. Only 15 of the 160 acres are planted for vineyards;
the rest are home to owls, hawks and other wildlife. Within
those 15 acres are five different sections that span more than a
half mile along the hillside. The sections are then divided into
half-acre blocks and planted according to the topography, soil
and microclimate. Cabernet Sauvignon is the dominating varietal, but there are several acres of Cabernet Franc, Merlot and
Petit Verdot.

"It's never the same if you impose your own will on something,"
says Jason. "It's like the winery: we don't want it to stick out
[of the landscape]. We want to be a part of it, not on top of it."

For the 2012 vintage, Jason will create one new single-vineyard
Cabernet, thanks to Futo's newly acquired site in Napa's Stags
Leap district. Its terrain is rocky, with hillside soil and terraced
old vines. The first vintage is in barrels now, and Jason believes
it lives up to his hopes for the site. The next step for the winery
is to refine, not expand.

Futo's reputation edges into greatness among appointed critics.
Its coveted 98-point score from the *Wine Advocate*'s founder,
Robert Parker Jr., has set a standard for its reputation. Jason
is particularly giddy over the crop from 2012, but forgoes early
celebration to focus on the tasks ahead. ❦

Futo
Winemaker: Jason Exposto
OAKVILLE, CA

Established 2002

Known for its Cabernet Sauvignon-based blend

Only produces about 1,000 cases annually

Wine is made solely from its estate

It employs a gravity-flow system to transport wine
within the winery

FutoWines.com

■

THE GOOD EARTH
Nicole has worked her way from assistant winemaker to winemaker
at Far Niente. She sees herself as a steward of the land, but she knows
the Far Niente brand will far outlast her term.

In the almost eight years since Nicole joined Far Niente, she has worked her way up from enologist, to assistant winemaker, to head winemaker. At Far Niente, Nicole's stewardship gives her purpose. She understands the well-established Far Niente brand doesn't revolve around her, and she likes to think there will be generations of Far Niente winemakers long after her. She says her role is to care for the brand, then pass it on. Understanding this bigger picture keeps her humble, despite Far Niente's popularity.

Home Improvement

While winemakers seem to have a complicated language of their own when talking about wine, Nicole feels that it shouldn't sway wine drinkers from exploring the world of wine. "Trust your palate" is her recommendation. "At a basic level, good is good. I don't think that you have to have a more informed palate to taste what 'good' is," says Nicole.

Far Niente has been "good" since 1885, and it has a weathered bottle of Far Niente Sweet Muscat from that vintage to prove it. The winery thrived until Prohibition; afterward, all that was left was its stone facade. In 1979, the Oklahomans Gil and Beth Nickel purchased the winery and vineyard and restored them both. During restoration, the phrase *far niente*, "without a care," was found engraved in stone at the winery entrance. In homage to its past, Far Niente still displays the building's engraving.

Nicole is responsible for maintaining Far Niente's "house style" while allowing an evolution of the wine based on vintage character, and improved farming and winemaking practices. About 35,000 cases are produced each year, and there are only two varieties: Cabernet Sauvignon and Chardonnay. The house style of the Cabernet is a richly layered palate with ripe fruit and finely integrated tannins. While approachable in its youth, Far Niente Cabernet is known to age for decades. Nicole believes the wines can be enjoyed alone or with a meal, with nuances all wine drinkers can taste.

Although she leads the winemaking at Far Niente, Nicole has many mentors and supporters. Far Niente has three sister wineries: Dolce, Nickel & Nickel and En Route. Nicole and her colleagues focus on different styles and varieties, but they're always sharing notes and talking through wine issues. Dirk Hampson, Far Niente's first winemaker, is the executive winemaking director and mentor to all the winemakers for the four houses in the family.

"Sometimes I can get caught up in the little things. Dirk helps me step back and view the big picture," says Nicole.

The company values its past, but it embraces change. For example, Far Niente's building is on the National Historic Register, but it's completely solar powered. In the winemaking department, Nicole's youthful energy keeps away cobwebs. As Far Niente adapts new winemaking and farming techniques, she tweaks the "house style" to reflect the changes. Inevitably, there's a lot riding on her decisions and her palate, but she likes the challenges. "Dirk gives you just enough rope to hang yourself with. If you make a mistake, it's on you. You've got to sink or swim," she says.

With the exception of harvest, most of Nicole's work takes place in the caves. It's a long walk down, which accounts for her fit physique. The caves, like any facility, have their challenges.

> "When I'm at work, I can't just turn off 'Nicole the Mom' and only be 'Nicole the Winemaker.' So, it becomes a creative balancing act."

Because there's no cell phone service, she and her team communicate using radios, the same way it was done when the caves were first built. In total, the caves measure the length of three football fields, and it covers 40,000 square feet. They were the first caves to be dug in North America in the twentieth century, designed in 1980 by the San Francisco tunnel engineer Alf Burtleson. Built as a practical solution to control the humidity and temperature during the winemaking process, they've become as popular as the collection of vintage race cars and high-octane motorcycles in the winery's adjoining carriage house.

Motherhood

Far Niente has been steadfast as Nicole became a bride and then a mother. Through these life changes, she has learned that neither motherhood nor career has to be sacrificed. But that

doesn't mean it's easy to combine them. At work, she's defined herself as a winemaker, but as a new mother she's challenged to incorporate the identity of "Mom", too.

"Trying to figure out how to be the best at your job and the best with your kids is a universal challenge for all working parents," says Nicole. "When I'm at work, I can't just turn off 'Nicole the Mom' and only be 'Nicole the Winemaker.' So, it becomes a creative balancing act."

Fortunately, her employers are family-friendly. She brought her baby boy, to harvest in 2011 when he was two months old. And as for sleep, it's "overrated", she claims.

In the workplace, motherhood has "forced" Nicole to be more organized and efficient with her time. It also has taught her perspective. Nicole oversees an oenologist, a cellar master, and a cellar crew, and most of them are parents, too. Nicole and

Far Niente was founded in 1885 by John Benson, who ventured west to participate in California's gold rush of 1849. It became decrepit after the Prohibition until Gil Nickel bought and restored the winery in 1979, and nurtured it into an iconic American brand.

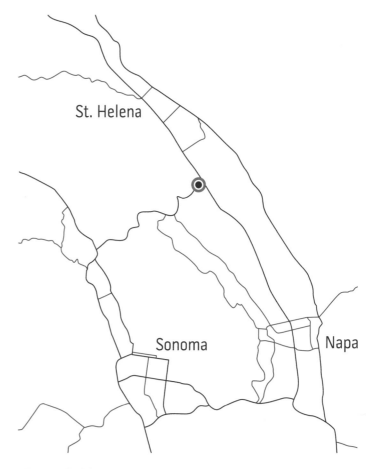

her colleagues' shared experience of parenthood has fostered a positive and supportive place to work. So, when family duty beckons, they all understand.

At home, she ruminates about wine and the outdoors with her husband, who's also a winemaker, and they hope to give their son an appreciation of their work as he grows older. Nicole brings home work when she needs to, and sometimes her son tags along when she wants to visit a few vineyards or stop by the office over the weekend. When she and her husband are overextended, their parents pitch in.

Nicole may work with her hands, but she hasn't lost her scholarly heart. Occasionally, she attends seminars at UC-Davis and becomes a student again. She enjoys absorbing the latest enological and viticultural research and looks for ways to incorporate it into the winemaking at Far Niente. Her long-term goals are the same as her goals for tomorrow: to make wines that represent Far Niente and to keep learning about wine.

"I have a secret to share about winemakers," she writes on Far Niente's blog. "We're really not as cool as you think we are. Deep down, we're just a bunch of geeks. Ok, so maybe we're a bunch of geeks who have the *really cool* job of making wine." 🍷

Far Niente
Winemaker: Nicole Marchesi
OAKVILLE, CA

....

Founded in 1885 and restored in 1979

Known for Cabernet Sauvignon and Chardonnay

Robert Whitley named Far Niente's 2008 Vintage "Wine of the Year," 2012

Buildings are solar powered, with 1,000 solar panels on pontoons floating in the winery's vineyard irrigation pond

First wine caves (40,000 ft^2) built in Napa since the 19th century

....

FarNiente.com

Far Niente floats solar panels on the vineyard's irrigation pond (photographed before solar panel addition.) The "floatovoltaic" system minimizes interruption to the land while serving as a conduit for the winery's solar power.

The Next Generation is in Business

SHANNON STAGLIN
President, Staglin Family Vineyard
Rutherford, CA

Shannon Staglin, President of Staglin Family Vineyard is a 34-year-old woman leading one of the most revered wineries in Napa. Many of Shannon's former Napa classmates are winemakers, but Shannon always saw herself in business management. Shannon prepared by obtaining an MBA from the UC-Davis Graduate School of Management, and developed business and marketing skills at Wells Fargo before returning to Staglin in 2011. In 2012, she was named its president, and her mother remains its CEO. Staglin Family Vineyard began in 1985, and they have raised and donated $725 million for research and treatment for mental health programs.

Q: How is Envolve Winery helping the industry as a whole? What do you think about their business model?

What they are doing for the wine industry as a whole is very important. Through their television celebrity, they are reaching a mainstream audience and introducing non-wine drinkers to wine and encouraging them to become wine consumers.

It's an effective marketing strategy which generates curiosity and will likely motivate many to become trail consumers of their products. With this type of exposure there is great promise for demand to exceed supply and as such they have successfully set themselves up for expansion. Although their business model is very different than at Staglin Family Vineyard, we do share one very important thing in common; people are a key component to the brand. Continued exposure, whether it be through TV or consumer events will be a key factor to their continued success and I think they are on the right track!

Q: What are the benefits of The Other Guys' business model?

With quality market research this has the potential to be a very successful business model. They are able to change swiftly, and if they can correctly predict future market trends, they can adapt and create a new brand that will resonate with the audience following these trends. Constant forward thinking is necessary and I would imagine this market segment is very competitive. I went to high school with both Donnie and Auggie; they are both dynamic and intelligent guys who will successfully carry on their family's legacy in wine while making their own generations mark in the industry.

Q: Why did your family decide to erect wine caves on its property?

Caves are the optimal environment for aging wine in barrels because they naturally provide an ideal temperature humidity level. With the humidity less wine is lost to evaporation and a steady cool temperature is integral to proper storage of wine.

Q: What business advice would you give to young emerging winemakers starting their own labels?

Their individual passion, energy, personality, ambition and consistent quality of their product will determine their success in the consumer market. It's important to network with others in the industry, as we are all dealing with the same labor of love, and can help each other reach our goals faster.

Q: How is managing a wine business, like Staglin Family Vineyards, different than any other industry?

The wine business is one of the last industries that is truly vertically integrated. At Staglin Family Vineyards, we manage every step of the process from the growing of the grapes, to the production of the wine to selling of the final product to the end consumer.

Family Roots Digging Deeper

Ceja Vineyards *DALIA CEJA*

Wagner Family Made Wine *JOE WAGNER*

Turley Wine Cellars *CHRISTINA TURLEY*

Ceja Vineyards

DALIA CEJA

At the age of twenty-seven, Dalia Ceja has stepped into a leading role in perpetuating the first Mexican-owned winery in Napa. Ceja Vineyards is one of the region's great stories of family achievement. Dalia leverages the brand's popularity to promote Hispanic culture with her fashionista flair and social media savvy. Making the most of her opportunity, she's studying for her master's in wine business and marketing, creating her first wine label, traveling the country selling Ceja, posing for magazines, and writing all about it on her blog, *The Ole! Report*.

2003   NAPA VALLEY · CARNEROS   Chardonn

Dalia attracts goodness like bees to the dahlia plant, her namesake. Dahlias populate the gardens in her mother's village of Las Flores in Jalisco, a state in western Mexico known for tequila and mariachi. Born with blonde hair and cat-green eyes, typical of Jalisco women and contrary to American perceptions, Dalia gushes family pride and enunciates every sentence with a lingering accent that works like an aphrodisiac on anyone within earshot.

The Ceja family struggled before they became financially successful, and it took thick-skinned persistence to achieve their goals. Hand-painted murals adorn their tasting room walls, connecting the history of winemaking with the Cejas' rise to the top, including their grandparents' march with César Chávez for better wages. Every bottle from the winery bears an image of a bell, symbolizing a "Celebration of Life" and the Cejas' fulfillment of the American Dream.

The Ceja story starts in the 1960s, when both sets of Dalia's grandparents settled in St. Helena, Napa, as emigrant farmworkers in Robert Mondavi's To Kalon vineyards and saved all their money to bring their children over the border. Dalia's mother, Amelia, and five siblings were living in Jalisco without electricity and water. Dalia's father, Pedro, was one of ten. After reuniting with their parents in California, Amelia and Pedro met each other in their teens at middle school.

"We went from vineyard workers to vineyard owners in a very short amount of time. Hard work, passion, and sacrifice were involved in building what is today Ceja Vineyards," says Dalia.

The Cejas bought their first property of 20 acres in 1982 in a region of Sonoma called Carneros. They soon expanded to 115 acres spanning Napa and Sonoma. Dalia grew up running around in the Chardonnay vineyards of Carneros with her brother, who owns a restaurant, Bistro Sabor, where he hosts weekly salsa nights. The Cejas are considered a Napa family, but Carneros,

"We went from vineyard workers to vineyard owners in a very short amount of time. Hard work, passion, and sacrifice were involved in building what is today Ceja Vineyards," says Dalia.

an appellation shared between Napa and Sonoma, is still their flagship vineyard. There they have recently renovated a mission-style winery equipped with hospitality spaces for fiestas.

"Inscribed on the bell on our bottles is 'Vinum. Cantus. Amor.' It means 'Wine. Song. Love.' But, if you were to talk to my dad he'd say it's 'wine, sex and rock 'n' roll,'" laughs Dalia.

Amelia Ceja is the president of Ceja, one of the first Latina women to hold that position in the American wine industry. Among many honors, she was named "Entrepreneur of the Year" by

Inc. Magazine and "Woman of the Year" by the California State Legislature in 2005. Dalia joined Ceja in 2009, and she's proud that three generations of women work at Ceja today. Her grandmother still helps around the gardens, kitchen, and vineyards.

"We are a women-run operation, but my dad is a very traditional Mexican Latin man and definitely has his opinions. At times, I want to pull my hair out. Still, we're doing something right, and we work well together," says Dalia.

Napa has been dominated by European and American men for

decades, but finally it's gaining some diversity. The Cejas were one of the first prominent Mexican families in Napa, and, slowly, other Mexican families are joining. In September 2012, the Cejas hosted Napa's second annual Mexican American vintners' fund-raising festival themed "Alianzas", Spanish for alliances. About a dozen vintners, representing the Napa–Sonoma Mexican-American Vintners Association, served wines as local restaurants provided food and mariachi roamed the grounds.

The average Ceja Vineyards annual production is a little under 10,000 cases. Keeping the production manageable allows the

Cejas to maintain a family-run business. They sell 80 percent of their grapes to other wineries.

Where Amelia is Ceja's chief and "chef," Dalia is its evangelist. Ceja educates drinkers in pairing Mexican cuisine with wine, for example, black beans with Cabernet. Dalia has been key to sharing the food-pairing experience by posting short messages and videos to Ceja's online community. She explains how tequila doesn't go with a chili because most tequila is too high in alcohol content; a drink with lower alcohol content and higher acidity, like wine, cuts through spice components. When her mom whips

up clam pasta or red snapper fish tacos, she Tweets to ask fans what wine they think will go best with those dishes. On Ceja's company website, Dalia's posted more than 150 three-minute video cooking lessons.

Belle of the Bottle

As the daughter of highly visible parents, Dalia sometimes feels overshadowed. To express herself, she started *The Ole! Report*, a blog about "food, fashion, wine, travel and fiesta." She's exploring opportunities outside the family business and can be seen in

various magazines and potentially a TV show called *The Faces and Winemakers of Napa Valley*, talking about wine and family with her typical, dramatic—yet relaxed—presence. She shares all of this in photo-based blog posts, meant to inspire *la bella vida*.

"For me, it gets a little hard. I have a dynamic family and gaining my own voice and character amidst a bundle of family members that already have huge success can be challenging," says Dalia.

Dalia inherited her parents' ingenuity for business and is honing her skills in an eighteen-month master's program on the wine

business and marketing. To stay on pace, Dalia carries around
textbooks and sets up makeshift study areas on sales trips and
in the tasting room. Her thesis assignment is to build a business
model, which goes hand in hand with Dalia's self-projected
future: starting her own wine label.

Naked Wines, one of the largest online wine retailers, recently
offered Dalia her own project wine label. The wines will be
sold to Naked Wines Angels, the company's investment group
funding up-and-coming winemakers like Dalia. The yearlong
process will be documented in an online video series, where her
investors can follow Dalia as she learns to make wine. Chances
are, the dusty vineyard soil won't stop her from wearing cowboy
boots and brightly colored outfits.

The label will be named La Tapatia, an endearing name describing
the fair-skinned women in Jalisco with *ojos Tapatios*, "fiery eyes."
The label will start with 2,500 cases of Chardonnay and about
3,000 cases of Pinot Noir. Dalia worked alongside experienced
winemakers and helped guide the ultimate style of the final
wines by doing punch downs and racking barrels, and she looks
forward to sharing the experience online with people unfamiliar
with how wine is produced. She'll continue working at Ceja as
she produces La Tapatia, but she knows she'll branch out more
permanently soon.

Dalia thinks a lot about her future, but for now she wants to
finish her master's degree, continue expanding her blog, and
take Ceja to the next level by "working the wine markets" as she
travels to promote the winery. Her ideal job would be to host an
entertainment show similar to Anthony Bourdain's *The Layover*,
where she could talk about wine, food, and fiestas around the
world, spiced up with a shot of international fashion. "But, I'll
always be a part of Ceja; it's in my blood." ♟♟

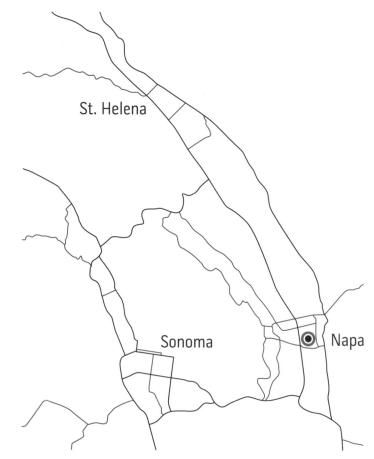

Ceja Vineyards
Sales and Marketing Director: Dalia Ceja
NAPA, CA

....

Established 2001

Known for Chardonnay, Pinot Noir and dessert wine
Dulce Besso, meaning "sweet kiss"

First Latino-owned winery in Napa

Developed more than 150 videos educating online
viewers about pairing wine with Mexican food

Dalia is making her first independent label,
"La Tapatia"

....

CejaVineyards.com

Wagner Family Made Wine

JOE WAGNER

When it comes to wine, Joe Wagner and his family have the magic touch. Joe is a fifth generation winemaker and comes from a family that has participated in various aspects of the wine business since the 1800s. Now, it's Joe's turn to contribute to the legacy. Joe independently started the Belle Glos Pinot Noir label that has taken the U.S. market by storm, and he also makes wine for Caymus Vineyards, which produces one of the world's most-recognized Cabernets.

All the Wagners will tell you there's no dividing line between their business and pleasure. It's all grapevines and wine. Joe's father and family patriarch, Chuck Wagner, often muses over farming techniques, winemaking nuances and the future of the wine business with his children. Working together as a family has continued to strengthen their bond, so much so that they jointly created an umbrella company named "Wagner Family Made Wine" that would solidify their family business and bring their successful wine ventures together as one.

The Son Also Rises

In 1972, Chuck and his parents, Charlie and Lorna, started the Wagners' flagship wine, Caymus Vineyards, on their Rutherford farm that they purchased in 1941. Charlie had been growing grapes on their home property from the onset and was tired of watching his fruit disappear into other wineries' bottles. He also

recognized that there was no longer a market for their primary crop of prunes and walnuts, and in order to support his family he would need to find another way to make ends meet. At age sixty, when most of Charlie's friends were retiring, he decided he could make better wines and more money by starting his own winery. Chuck was just a teenager and hadn't yet developed a taste for wine, but he fully supported his parent's decision and chose to join them in their new venture.

The Wagners' chose "Caymus" as the name of their Rutherford vineyard, which refers to an 1836 Mexican land grant in the Napa Valley. The family produced their first wines in 1972—Pinot Noir, German-style Riesling, and the now iconic Cabernet Sauvignon. Charlie was a strong-willed farmer who was rarely seen without a straw hat and suspenders, and he had a vision for the future of Napa Valley's wine business. The Wagners quickly gained a loyal following and respect when its Cabernet Sau-

Belle Glos, adorned with a smooth, burgundy-colored wax closure, is Joe's interpretation of Pinot Noir with authentic California character.

■
FATHERING A BRAND

Joe Wagner is father to five children, but he maintains focus as founder of Meiomi and Belle Glos, and winemaker at Caymus.

vignon started winning awards, so they decided to focus solely on that variety. Notably, Charlie and Chuck's Caymus Special Selection Cabernet is the only wine to have twice won the *Wine Spectator* magazine's prestigious "Wine of the Year" Award.

Chuck is still the head winemaker at Caymus Vineyards, and is now proud to have his children working alongside him. Starting in elementary school, Joe and his three siblings were strongly encouraged to help out in Caymus' vineyards so they could "learn the ropes by doing".

While all of the Wagners now have their own independent niches in the family business, Joe has also taken on a significant wine-making role for Caymus. Joe's older brother, Charlie II, makes two Chardonnays: Mer Soleil Barrel Fermented and Mer Soleil Unoaked Silver. Silver is bottled in gray-sheen ceramic bottles, mimicking the cement tanks Charlie II uses to ferment his wine. Both labels are produced in Monterey County, California, on land the Wagners have been planting with vines since in the late 1980s. Joe's younger sister Jenny is an apprentice winemaker at Caymus. Her brothers convinced her to start making her own wine and Jenny began experimenting with Sauvignon Blanc and Merlot, and her first release of Sauvignon Blanc appeared in Caymus' tasting room in 2012. Erin, the youngest, is attending college but has put her fair share of summertime hours into the family business.

Building a Case (Many Cases) for Pinot Noir

In 2001, at age nineteen, Joe decided to seriously practice viti-culture, so he quit his studies at the Brooks Institute of Photography and began working at a 400-acre table grape vineyard in northern Mexico. Originally, Joe wasn't sure whether he wanted to work for Caymus full-time, but he quickly formed an attachment to the business. He started earning his keep in vineyard management and crossed over to winemaking.

"Hard work is the key element to success. If you are driven to learn every aspect of the business and work as hard as you can, it will be a successful brand."

As Joe became engrossed in winemaking, he started his own Pinot Noir label—Belle Glos—named in honor of his paternal grandmother Lorna Belle Glos Wagner, and her love for Pinot Noir.

Prior to the release of the blockbuster movie *Sideways*, Pinot Noir was often considered too feminine for the male drinker. Most of the California winemaking techniques used to make Pinot Noir in the early 2000s created what Joe called "undrinkable wines," but he knew there was potential for the variety. In 2002, Joe was so confident in the quality of his Pinot Noir grapes that he risked his budding reputation and increased Belle Glos' production three-fold. To him, it was worth "betting the farm" in order to avoid selling such an asset on the bulk market. *Sideways* came out shortly after the vintage was released, and the wine sold within a matter of months.

"It was really interesting to see the market dynamics change. Demand increased for the varietal, so Pinot Noir producers started making better wines that offered greater value to consumers," he says.

Within one year after the movie's 2004 release, retail sales for the variety increased exponentially. Belle Glos, adorned with a smooth, burgundy-colored wax closure, is Joe's interpretation of Pinot Noir with authentic California character. Each single-vineyard bottle is made with grapes from one of three California counties: Monterey, Santa Barbara or the Sonoma Coast.

Belle Glos' other label, Meiomi (pronounced *May-oh-me*,) was created to satisfy restaurants' sudden demand for a twenty dollar Pinot Noir. It started as Belle Glos' "Sonoma Coast" label in 2002, and then in 2006, he rebranded it as a separate label and named it "Meiomi", meaning "coastal" in the native language of the Californian Wippo tribe. Joe applies many of the philosophies he learned at Caymus to Meiomi, particularly the process of blending grapes from various sites to create consistent flavors. As a result, Meiomi is a blend of more than two-dozen carefully selected vineyards spread across what he considers to be the best cool-climate areas of California's coast. Currently, it's one of the best-selling Pinot Noirs in the country.

"Hard work is the key element to success. If you are driven to learn every aspect of the business and work as hard as you can, it will be a successful brand."

While Chuck supports his son's business, he still has exacting expectations that might seem overbearing to those outside the family. "Don't mess it up" is a fond saying of Chuck's that still rings loudly in Joe's ears. Joe maintains that his father never expected Belle Glos or Meiomi to be as successful as they are now, but Joe has built a Pinot Noir powerhouse. Within the last year, Belle Glos and Meiomi have more than doubled in sales. Meiomi is the best-selling Pinot Noir in its price class, while Belle Glos ranks as one of the top overall 20 luxury wines (wine costing more than 20 dollars) in the nation. There is no doubt that Joe is ushering in a golden generation for Pinot Noir in America.

Great Expectations

Beyond Pinot Noir, Joe is one of three Cabernet Sauvignon winemakers at Caymus, and they all practice independent site and fermentation management, preferring to keep their practices and winemaking decisions under wraps until their annual post-vintage blind tasting and review. It is an exercise intended to create healthy competition within their ranks, ultimately motivating each winemaker to create something exceptional. "This approach has proven to be an effective way

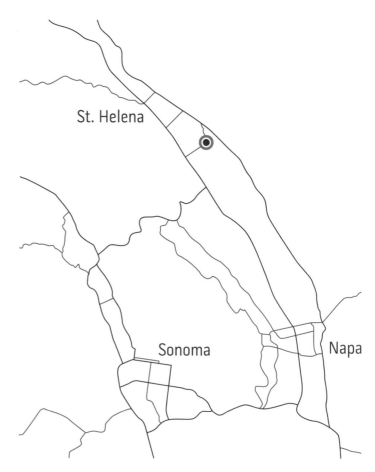

to fast-track continued development and improvements to our winemaking and grape growing techniques. It's our homegrown spin on research and development," says Joe.

To create the Caymus blend, they must taste wines from seventy different vineyard lots, from eight of Napa Valley's sixteen sub-appellations. Chuck insists on blind tasting exercises, forcing each team member to constantly study and improve their wine-making process. Approximately one quarter of the lots never make the high quality standard for the Caymus label and are sold to other producers.

"There is no such thing here as the *status quo*. We think there are always more opportunities and answers, so we push the envelope to find them. We've had as many failures as we have successes. It's the ability to learn from missteps and build on successes that keeps you on the right track," says Joe.

Continuing the Legacy

Joe and his wife Amber have five young children, but when it comes to harvest, he has no qualms about sleeping at the winery. "It can be hard, but everyone's got to suck it up and put the work in," says Joe. "Harvest is when you make all the decisions that are key to the wine's quality for that vintage."

At home, with Joe and Amber's guidance, their kids are already experimenting with fermentation science, making wines in five-gallon plastic Igloo containers. Soon, Joe will send the kids out into the fields for some honest work like his dad did with him, and by demonstrating his zeal and dedication, he hopes to encourage them to continue the tradition of another father-son (or daughter) winemaking team. 🍷

Wagner Family Made Wine
Winemaker: Joe Wagner
NAPA VALLEY, CA

....

Caymus established 1972

Also owns two award-winning Pinot Noir labels: Meiomi and Belle Glos

Joe is a fifth generation winemaker

Makes three of the top 20 luxury-priced ($20+) wines in the United States

Meiomi won #1 Pinot Noir in 2012 by *Wine & Spirits Magazine*

....

WagnerFamilyofWine.com

Turley Wine Cellars

CHRISTINA TURLEY

Christina Turley, twenty-eight, has the urban savvy of a Trump and the self-possession of a Kennedy. She stores wine bottles in her oven and ages her own Negroni cocktails in a two-gallon barrel on her kitchen counter. And as the face of Turley Wine Cellars, she aims to create an "American" wine culture through Zinfandel, thereby sweeping away the stereotypes that have gathered around the varietal like dust bunnies.

■

NEWCOMERS

Christina Turley is shepherding two new Turley wines into the industry:
a white Zinfandel and a Cabernet Sauvignon. The Cabernet, as seen on
the left, is sold as a new brand called The Label.

Many uninformed biases have clustered around Zinfandel grapes and Turley Wine Cellars since Christina's father, Larry Turley, founded the company in 1993. Larry started Turley hot off the heels of his first—and highly successful—wine venture, Frog's Leap. He and his partner John Williams built a prestigious reputation for organic farming and the wines it produced. When Frog's Leap outgrew Larry's interests, he transferred his love for organic and dry-farmed vineyards to his eponymous brand in Napa and focused in on Zinfandel, especially the old-vine Zinfandel that Turley is now known for.

Larry's sister, Helen, was the first winemaker. She was already an icon, so their first wines were dissected by both critics and consumers like a frog in a middle school science lab.

Christina oversees Turley's national sales and still hears many speculations during trips to host tastings and dinners. Many think her aunt still makes the wine (Helen left in 1995), while others think Helen is Christina's mom. On the road, Christina often runs into stubborn drinkers who refuse to drink Turley or Zinfandel, claiming the wines are "hot," "fruity," "jammy," "flabby," or "one-noted." Her ears prick up in defense whenever she encounters these terms; and generally, with a little coaxing, the naysayers venture into unknown territory, try a few sips, and become brownnosing enthusiasts.

"I hear the phrase *fruit bomb* all the time. Last night I was at a consumer tasting, and one guy told me that the Turley Zinfandel was a fruit bomb. I started arguing with him, thinking he was disrespecting the wine, until he actually said that he meant *fruit bomb* in a good way," says Christina.

Rosé-Colored Glasses

Christina is plowing forward with new projects that she describes as not "in keeping with what people expect." Turley has long been known for its Petite Syrah and Zinfandel, and

Christina believes it's time to push some boundaries. She has no qualms about asking for what she wants—white Zinfandel. It's always had a cheap reputation, but Christina refuses to let its potential lie fallow. It took a year for the Turley team to acquiesce to the first vintage of 2011 Turley white Zinfandel, which sold out in an hour.

Christina decided not to label it as a white Zinfandel or a Zinfandel rosé; it's simply red Zinfandel grapes picked early. Similarly, the bottle doesn't make any claims: it just says "Zinfandel," printed in gold lettering on a crisp white label. It's made more like white wine, dry and acidic, than the typically sweet white Zinfandels of the past. When sommeliers put the white-label Turley Zinfandel on their wine list, it's up to them to decide if they want to call it white Zinfandel or Zinfandel rosé; others just skip this decision and hand-sell it.

The wine is made in the style of Zinfandel rosé in Provence, France. While there are other high-end brands that make it in the Provençal-style, no one calls it a white Zinfandel. Christina uses the term purposely, in an attempt to reclaim both the term and the wine itself from its sordid past. It's all part of Turley's goal to create a home-team culture for the Zinfandel varietal.

"We can make Pinot Noir until the cows come home, but it will never be Burgundy. And we're never going to be Bordeaux. Instead of comparing ourselves to the Old World, let's embrace where we are and what we have to offer," says Christina.

Grapes for the white label come from the same vines as those used for Turley's estate red Zinfandel. But the clusters are picked about a month earlier and spend less time "on the skins" during fermentation. Zinfandel is known to be a "finicky" thin-skinned grape, but it does very well for the Turleys and many other vintners in California.

"It's arguably the closest thing you'll get to an indigenous variety

in California. It is technically related to a Croatian grape, Crljenak Kaštelanski, but over the years it's changed and become its own entity in California. It's not made the same way anywhere else in the world," says Christina.

A Sommelier's Satisfaction

Christina has also become her own entity. As the oldest child of two, she has many firstborn characteristics that reinforce her ability to lead. When she was young, her parents divorced and

her mother retained custody, so Christina didn't have regular interaction with her father or his burgeoning wine business. After her dad remarried, Christina gained two younger half sisters whom she saw on weekends. At fifteen, she asked to leave Redwood High School in Marin, for boarding school.

At Redwood, Christina slept through her classes, but still received good grades. It wasn't socially acceptable to try hard, which annoyed her. She knew that she needed smaller, academically rigorous classes, which she found at Cate School

"It was my epiphany moment. It was the first real food and wine pairing experience that really made sense," says Christina.

in Santa Barbara. Christina moved even farther away for college, to New York University and then Barnard College in Manhattan, where she graduated with an art history degree in 2006. She thrived in Barnard's challenging urban environment and had no intentions of leaving the east coast.

From the time Christina could legally drink until 2008, she helped her dad at annual Turley portfolio tastings at the Metropolitan Pavilion in New York City. It was their way of staying in touch despite living on separate coasts, and they often caught up over dinner once the day was over.

One of those dinners was at Momofuku Ssäm bar on Second Avenue, where the manager served the Turleys thick meats paired with high-acid white wines. Given the Turley family's preference for big red wines with meat, Christina was surprised that it tasted right. That meal sparked her interest in working at Momofuku, and she started as a sommelier soon after.

"It was my epiphany moment. It was the first real food and wine pairing experience that really made sense," says Christina.

Christina was promoted to lead sommelier at Momofuku Ssäm's sister restaurant, Ko, but she didn't pretend to know what she was doing. She was honest about her amateur status. David Chang took a chance on her, as he does with many young upstarts, but it helped that she was "a Turley." Her inexperience

became her strength. She never assumed that mushrooms had to go with Burgundy or, like her first experience, that red meats had to pair with heavy Cabernets.

"One night, we did a chilled light-red Trousseau wine with a dish that tasted like the forest, but very subtly—hand-torn noodles, matsutake mushrooms, pine nuts, broth, and chives that looked like pine needles. It was like eating the forest," says Christina. "The somewhat spicy, lightly aromatic Trousseau, a lighter cousin to Pinot Noir, was perfect, and very well received."

Unexpected Moves

In 2010, Turley's general manager and director of winemaking, Ehren Jordan, urged Christina to come home and work for the family business. Turley Wine had just acquired new Cabernet vineyards, and he wanted her to direct and design a new label separate from the Turley brand. The long-term benefits were clear, and Christina moved back to St. Helena, Napa, within six weeks. Nine months later, in the middle of label design and fine-tuning the branding strategy, Turley's national sales director left. Ehren invited Christina to fill the position, and she accepted.

After only a few years at Turley, Christina's influenced major changes. She's overseen two new projects, the Turley white Zinfandel and a Cabernet Sauvignon enigmatically called "The Label." The Label harks back to the winemaking style of

TURLEY
WINE CELLARS
MINER
PRESTON
OF DRY CREEK
SAINTSBURY
LOVE the ZIN
you're IN

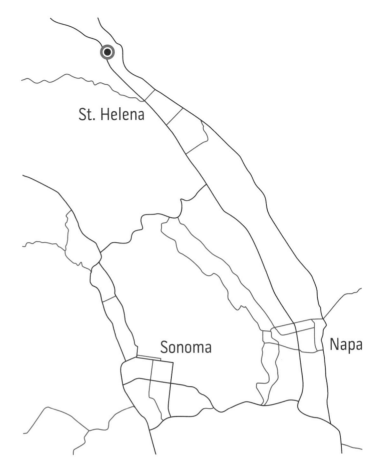

the 1970s, with lower alcohol levels, herbal notes, and austere tannins. And the label itself reflects Christina's penchant for artful modernism.

The Next Chapter

At her very core, Christina's a city girl. It's taken two years to adjust to the quiet countryside in St. Helena, and she still misses the east coast. She's used to the fast talking, fast walking, and fast working pace of Manhattan's sommelier scene. Christina was surrounded by supportive friends and constant urban activity; loneliness was a new and unwelcome feeling that settled in like fog for more than two years after the move. Until last year, Christina had few friends besides her sisters. When she's asked what she did during the first two years back in St. Helena, she always says the same thing, with a loud sigh. "I cried."

Now, "thankfully," Christina has her group of like-minded friends; and, after two years of being single, an international boyfriend, with whom she shares weekend rendezvous that include wine tastings in Budapest and Paris.

The struggles of her transition to wine country will soon be well documented in her first authored book. She scribbles ideas for it in between distributor dinners and sales travels. Christina can easily turn out Turley's newsletters with smart prose, but self-reflective writing is a different matter. When the introduction proved daunting to write, she quickly changed her focus to her "rainbows and unicorns" twenty-eighth birthday party: oysters on the half shell, champagne, bone marrow pizza, and rainbow carrots made by her sister Savannah and shared with 15 friends.

"It will be a younger *Eat, Pray, Love*," says Christina. "But with way more booze." 🍷

Turley Wine Cellars
National Sales Manager: Christina Turley
TEMPLETON, CA

....

Established 1993

Known for Zinfandel and Petite Syrah

Two-year waiting list to buy Turley's single vineyard wines

Christina was responsible for the design and marketing of a Cabernet Sauvignon, part of new brand called *The Label*

....

TurleyWineCellars.com

A Restaurateur's Perspective

DENNIS KELLY
Master Sommelier at The French Laundry
Yountville, California

Dennis Kelly, The French Laundry's Head Sommelier, is responsible for managing the restaurant's wine program, complementing its celebrated nine-course menu. With rare instinct, he personalizes the wine and food pairing experience for each dinner table, and mentors his sommelier team in the same craft. With more than a decade of experience, as well as a title from the Court of Master Sommeliers, Dennis maintains a unique on-the-pulse perspective of the world of wine and its consumers.

Dennis speaks to author Chelsea Prince about the art of creating distinctive wines in an international wine market:

Q: How can California winemakers compete against international and Old World wines?

The most important thing that any winemaker can do is to make balanced wines that show a 'sense of place.' California offers incredible natural resources and diversity, and the finest California winemakers take full advantage of these qualities.

Q: What is your opinion on biodynamic farming?

I like many of the biodynamic principles philosophically, but there are countless quality-driven producers that utilize "organic viticulture" or even "lutte raisonnée" to make incredible wines. I think that all these practices reflect a desire to farm sustainably and produce the finest wine possible, and that the most prestigious names in wine subscribe to one of these three approaches.

Q: Do gravity-flow systems create the best quality wines?

My understanding is that gravity-flow systems are particularly advantageous for Pinot Noir producers, because the thin-skin grape is so transparent. The pressure of pumps can negatively affect this delicate grape, so 'gravity-flow' is quite popular in Oregon, New Zealand and Burgundy, where there have been a lot of new developments to improve the quality of Pinot Noir.

Q: What are the benefits of half bottles?

At The French Laundry we offer more than 300 selections in the 375ml format. Based on our multi-course menu format, half-bottles allow our guests to enjoy a progression of wines with their meal. It's all about the right format in the right situation, and a variety of options is a huge advantage.

Q: There are very few wine families left in Napa and Sonoma. Why do we have few family wineries left, and does it matter? Do you think that families are selling out too early?

This has been an issue for family wineries throughout the world for decades. In Germany, Italy and France for example, children go away to cities to study and find other interests besides the family winery. Ultimately, they often prefer to inherit a fortune than the family wine business, so they follow their own dreams. The family eventually has to sell the business without a family member to carry on the tradition. It's a sad reality, but it is a very common problem.

The lifestyle in Napa and Sonoma is generally more appealing to young family members than the Mittelrhein in Germany, so it's actually less of an issue here than in many other places throughout the world.

Q: How do you personalize the wine pairings for each dinner table at The French Laundry?

We believe that it is important to consider our guest's preferences when selecting wines to accompany his or her meal. We want to know whether the host is open to international selections, or if they prefer to imbibe local wines. We also consider stylistic preferences, the quantity of wine preferred and budgetary guidelines. Frequently, our guests simply put the decision making in our hands. In this case, we do our best to create a symbiotic relationship between food and wine in order to elevate the dining experience to a level even greater than the sum of its parts.

Transitioning into New Clones

Bedrock Wine *MORGAN TWAIN-PETERSON*

The Other Guys *AUGUST SEBASTIANI*

Dark Matter *ANGELINA MONDAVI*

Bedrock Wines

MORGAN TWAIN-PETERSON

Though many winemakers focus on what's new, Morgan
Twain-Peterson rehabilitates old vines to venerate the past.
He studies the land and cares for it like a gardener pruning
a rosebush. He's the history keeper—the preserver of old
Sonoma vines and tall tales. And nobody tells the story of
wine like Morgan.

"Whole Cluster
Carneros
Syrah

20
08

Leave it to Morgan Twain-Peterson to make old-vineyard history more entertaining than a primetime television show. He's a connoisseur with a teacher's attitude and a master vintner's palate. Morgan made his first wine, the 1986 Vino Bambino Pinot Noir, at the ripe old age of five. He asked for grapes with the intention of making a wine equal to those of France's Domaine de la Romanée-Conti, a name most five-year-olds can't even pronounce. Now thirty-one, Morgan has released his first public brand, Bedrock Wine Co., which is as layered with flavors as it is with scurrilous California history.

The Bedrock brand is named after his father's first vineyard purchase, Bedrock Vineyard, where Morgan sources and farms many of his grapes. The vineyard, formerly part of Madrone Ranch, has been passed down and broken up through northern California's most influential and, often, notorious men.

After the Mexican–American War ended and the 1849 Gold Rush simmered down, William Tecumseh Sherman and Joseph Hooker bought the six-hundred-acre Madrone Ranch and started farming. Sherman funded the purchase and the property's operation, as long as Hooker managed and planted the property, which he did haphazardly. They parted ways after rancorous debates over the state of the property, and their feud extended into the Civil War. Sherman, who became a Union Army general, made sure to stiff Union Major General "Fightin' Joe" Hooker to avenge his lost vineyard investment. While Hooker wasn't much use as a farmer, he was effective at inspiring his army by bringing bands of courtesans to travel with the officers. The men howled with delight at the rare sight of women, but when any officer tried to approach Hooker's private harem, he was stopped in his tracks. "No, you can't have those. Those are Hooker's."

"That's where the term *hooker* comes from," declares Morgan.

Continuing a Legacy

Back to the future and years later, Madrone Ranch was sold to the Italian Parducci and Domenici families. Another vineyard

The vineyard, formerly part of Madrone Ranch, has been passed down and broken up through northern California's most influential and, often, notorious men.

conflict arose, and the two families split their three-hundred-acre parcel in half. Joel Peterson, Morgan's father, purchased the Domenici portion in 2004 and renamed it Bedrock.

Joel, the founder of Ravenswood, is known as Sonoma's hippie-liberal godfather of Zinfandel. For a young man such as Morgan, a father's success can be daunting. Joel sold Ravenswood to the world's largest wine company, Constellation Brands, for 147 million dollars. He's still working, as Constellation's senior vice president, and was recently inducted into the Vintners Hall of Fame at the Culinary Institute of America. So it would be no surprise to see Morgan work in an industry that has no affiliation with nature, Sonoma, or wine. Instead, Morgan celebrates his dad's successes with a wine label in his honor.

When Morgan was about to graduate with a master's in American studies from Columbia University, his dad called to announce the purchase of a Sonoma vineyard. Ravenswood operated entirely on purchased fruit, so this was a personal purchase—Joel's first after thirty years in the industry. Morgan assumed it was a small vineyard with a few blocks to toy around with. Instead, it was 119 acres with 33 acres of very special, old vines planted before 1955.

"It's the old Madrone Ranch," said Joel. Morgan knew exactly what land his dad was describing. He knew it had more than twenty interplanted varieties: Zinfandel, Syrah, Barbera, esoteric white grapes, and two blocks of Carignane and Mourvèdre planted in 1888. At least he had a place to work if he didn't pur-

sue a doctorate. After Morgan watched a few bright peers settle for professorships in Podunk towns, he opted for the vineyard.

"This is living history. It's a lot more fun," he says.

Morgan is co-owner of Bedrock Vineyard with his father and stepmother, and also works with twenty-three other vineyards. Although he makes more than thirty different wines, he focuses on small quantities because most of the fruit comes from low-yielding old vines. His label Bedrock produces only 4,000 cases of wine annually.

He also sells another 4,000 cases of a wine called "Shebang", a blend of grapes that don't go into the Bedrock labels. His Bedrock wines are carefully crafted yet affordable (less than 39 dollars) and sell almost entirely to his mailing list of 2,700 people. Two thousand people are waiting to join the list, but Morgan has no intention of making more wine to satisfy the demand. By keeping production manageable, he does what he loves best: farm and study old-vine vineyards.

Venerating Vineyard History

Sonoma is a rare haven for old vines. With burly, gnarled trunks and sprawling willow-like branches, old vines are easy to spot. They're often unevenly plotted, seeming to zigzag through the vineyard. Old vines look haunting when bare, with stocky legs and a Medusa-like head.

The first time Morgan knew his father's wine brand, Ravenswood, was growing was during a movie theatre showing of *Fear and Loathing in Las Vegas*. In the middle of the movie, someone in the aisle behind him passed him down a bottle of Ravenswood Vintners Blend and offered a swig.

"One thing I do love about old vineyards is that you don't get uniformity—the vines themselves are habitats for salamanders and bugs because they live in the crevices of the bark. You get more of a full ecosystem in the vineyard, which I always like, except when I happen upon a snake," says Morgan, who finds lurking snakes wound around his old vines in Monte Rosso's Rattlesnake Hill.

Morgan is a self-proclaimed wine nerd who considers learning a perpetual work in progress. Last year, he submitted a dissertation on old vines to qualify for the internationally esteemed status of Master of Wine. It's known as the most rigorous wine test in the world, issued by the Institute of Masters of Wine in the United Kingdom, and conceived in the 1950s. The four-day exam is given in Napa, London and Sydney. Only about three hundred Masters of Wine exist worldwide, with an average of eight people passing every year. To qualify to take the exam, each applicant must complete two years of coursework, subsequent blind-tasting exams, essays on wine markets and varietals, and the 10,000-word dissertation. Morgan didn't pass, nor did any of his American peers. "Harvest started before I received the results, so luckily I was distracted," said Morgan. He'll have two more tries to receive a passing score.

Morgan harvests his grapes like vintners of generations past by bringing in his field blends all at once, and he makes wine with traditional hands-on methods to enhance the natural flavors. He pitchforks his grapes into a stainless steel destemmer, then pumps them into open-top fermenters where native yeasts do the work. To complete punch downs, he stands on a two-by-eight wooden plank above the fermenting tank and manually pushes down the thick, floating layer of grape skins and seeds with a metal "punch," or plunger.

In the wine industry it's popular to harvest and ferment varieties separately. Morgan's approach bucks the trend.

"I usually just coferment everything. I figure the vines are planted there for a reason," he says.

Embedded in each of Morgan's wines is a history lesson. Morgan is known for his "heritage wines", made from a natural blend of up to twenty varieties. He uses an abstract name rather than a varietal description on the label to engage his customers in the wine's true makeup. The technique of blending handfuls of varieties isn't obscure or new. Until the 1960s, Morgan says the variety was secondary to what California winemakers were trying to achieve. By interplanting varieties, often as many as eleven in one block, winemakers could create what they thought was the most complete wine. It also created a safety net, so at least some grapes each harvest performed well.

"They didn't have all of the tools we have in the modern winery to create fine blends. Most of the blending happened in the field," says Morgan.

When Morgan finds a grape cluster he's never seen before, he sends it to a lab at the University of California at Davis. By cross-referencing the grape's or leaf's DNA, he's found varieties that are essentially extinct everywhere else in the world. Over the last three years, Morgan and his peers with similar old-vine interests have sent approximately sixty samples to UC-Davis. Four samples came back with no DNA match. Several others, like Castets, Mollard and Feher Szagos are nonexistent in their home regions.

"This is living history. It's a lot more fun," he says.

BEDF
20 08

Morgan opens bottles of Bedrock moments before his annual harvest party begins. He invites family, close friends and colleagues to celebrate the culmination of harvest with bluegrass music, oysters and pig roasted on a spit.

To raise public awareness of historic California vineyards, Morgan and five old-vine allies started the Historic Vineyard Society. Established in 2010, the nonprofit's mission is to educate the wine-drinking public on the dwindling number of old vines and the importance of preservation. The society's officers maintain a registry of historic vineyards with up-to-date, online notifications of recent additions and partnerships with other organizations around the world.

Morgan is doing his share to revitalize old vineyards. He recently leased a problematic vineyard established in 1905 and is now pruning to bring its vigor back. The vineyard is missing 67 percent of its vines, so Morgan is tending to it with the current vineyard manager to bring it back to full production. Morgan is dry-farming the vines and teaching the new manager how to properly care for century-old vines.

Sometimes working with historic vines in a town with few young people can make one feel rather old. This year, Morgan's friend, Chris Cottrell, who at age twenty-seven and looks at least ten years older than Morgan, is moving from New York City to join Bedrock, primarily to help Morgan start a sparkling wine brand. "Chris knows more about wine than anyone should," laughs Morgan.

Morgan and Chris are going to make the first vineyard-designated récoltant-manipulant-style sparkling wines in California. Many sparkling wines are a blend of grapes. It's a concept used by most large Champagne houses including Taittenger Comtes de Champagne, the first liquid to touch Morgan's lips at birth. They'll be making two types: Blanc de Blancs, an ultralight sparkling wine made from Chardonnay, and a red bubbly made in Lambrusco style from old-vine Zinfandel, with low alcohol and earthy aromas. They'll produce about 100 cases from each vineyard. Morgan has no experience with sparkling wine and anticipates a challenge, but he hopes progress will come naturally. 🍷🍷

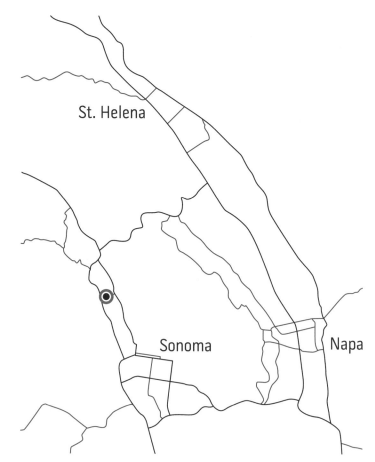

Bedrock Wines
Winemaker: Morgan Peterson
SONOMA, CA

....

Established 2007

Known for "heirloom" wines, Syrah, Cabernet Sauvignon, Zinfandel, Pinot Noir, Rose, Bordeaux Blanc Blends

Morgan's father is Joel Peterson, founder of Ravenswood Winery

Proponent of ancient vines

Co-founder of the Historical Vineyard Society

....

BedrockWineCo.com

The Other Guys

AUGUST SEBASTIANI

August Sebastiani is already one of the wine industry's most savvy businessmen, anchoring another generation of Sebastiani success in the wine business without touching a single vineyard. The Other Guys, his new company, sells about 300,000 cases annually. His eyes are now on the liquor and craft beer industries, and it'll be no surprise to see him conquer them, too.

LEESE - FIT

LEESE-FITCH ADO
MISSION SAN FR
SOLANO. BUILT I

CABERNET
SAUVIGNON

SE - FITC

August Sebastiani lives blocks away from winemaker Morgan Twain-Peterson of Bedrock Wine Co. in Sonoma, but August's niche in the wine industry couldn't be more different. They're both born to fathers with legacies in the wine business, but where Morgan keeps his wine production down so he can tend to his old-vine vineyards, August stays out of the vineyard so he can sell more wine.

August, nicknamed "Aug", was born in 1980 into the fourth-generation of one of Sonoma's most storied wine families. He didn't, however, inherit the Sebastiani family green thumb. Aug isn't alone; his older brother Donny and younger sister Mia are also business hounds, not farming folk. Mia is focusing on food–wine pairings and has started her own line of pasta sauces and olive oils that complement wines. Donny runs Don Sebastiani & Sons, a wine negociant company that perpetuates the family name and tradition. In 2005, the *Wine Enthusiast* named the company "American Winery of the Year".

The Sebastiani facilities were Aug's playground throughout his childhood, and he found ample opportunities to learn. Then, in high school Aug spent summers working in the mailroom and the purchasing department. He made weekly mail runs to Lodi, where he'd drive two hours to check in at the winery, grab a sandwich at a local shop, and drive back. After proving his dedication, Aug was allowed to work with customers in the tasting room in Sonoma.

Numerous family members took turns running Sebastiani Vineyards, but Aug remembers his dad, Don, at the helm most of his life. Don took over for his brother Sam in 1985 and, within fifteen years, brought production from two million to almost eight million cases. February 15, 2001, two years before Aug graduated college, Don Sebastiani sold off the Lodi winery and about 8 million cases of table wine to Constellation, currently the largest wine and spirits holding group in the United States.

"It was too tough finding blue sky for everyone," says Aug.

In 2004, when Don felt his sons were mature, he inaugurated them into the business. Don started Don Sebastiani & Sons to prime his sons to lead the next generation in wine. Mia was still too young to join then, but Don, Donny Jr., and Aug became joint partners. Their business is known for the labels Smoking Loon and Pepperwood Grove. Others in the nine-brand portfolio include Aquinas, The Crusher and Don & Sons.

Aug's primary venture, The Other Guys, started in 2004 as a distribution company (with the same name) in northern California. Aug and his business associates had a couple trucks delivering Don Sebastiani & Sons wine and ended up bringing on others' brands to distribute, too. After too many hours on the road, Aug lost the appetite to spend Fridays driving cases of Hey Mambo to Monterey, and they hadn't attained critical mass. Over the next few years they transitioned into the formal company known as The Other Guys. In 2009, The Other Guys completely separated from Don Sebastiani & Sons and branded themselves with the tagline "Laid-back guys, stand-out wines." Aug's aim is to adapt the Sebastiani business to the next generation, turning the "next page" of one of California's oldest wine businesses.

"I find our wine and spirits to be more playful than what's out there. There has been too much stuffiness in the wine business," says Aug.

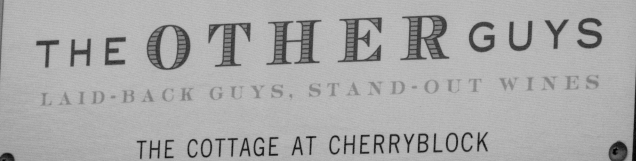

Sense & Sensibility: Wines, Spirits and Craft Beer

Aug describes The Other Guys (TOG) as a brand marketing and sales company. Donny, Mia and Aug are the proprietors, and Aug is at the helm as President. They're approaching their business very differently from their great-grandfather, Samuele, who was a grape grower. Samuele ran his small winery during the Prohibition, and was one of only seven in the state of California to continue to produce wine—for medical and religious purposes. Post-Prohibition, Samuele's son August ran the company and he would transport Sebastiani grapes via train to Chicago, where he had no say in how or where the juice was bottled. Aug starts on the other end. He forecasts what wines will sell well in the market; picks out the bottles, the labels, and the price points; and, finally, finds the best-suited grape-growing production

partners to work with. In 2011, TOG sold 40 percent more wine than in 2010, and Aug expects to double sales again between 2012 and 2013.

Aug makes decisions based on what sells well, depending on the DNA and margins of each brand. He's bullish on craft beer and is interested in expanding his spirits portfolio. In 2012, TOG added four new labels under its new craft beverage company called 35 Maple Street: three premium spirits brands and an IPA named "Gus the Bus" after Aug's youngest child. Gus the Bus is sold locally as a way to test the market and build grassroots traction. Many craft brews, like Anchor Steam, Racer 5 IPA and Lagunitas were born in northern California, and Aug is eager to participate in the movement.

Nonetheless, wine is still 98 percent of The Other Guys' business, and Aug is very happy with where the company is headed in terms of providing diversity to its distributors. He describes TOG as a one-stop-shop for small distributors and restaurants looking for a handful of offerings at affordable price points. TOG stands as a middleman between the producers and the consumers. Leese-Fitch is their flagship brand, at about 160,000 cases, followed by Hey Mambo and Plungerhead, about 300,000 cases combined. Hey Mambo's flavor names like Kinky Pink, Swanky White and Sultry Red, and other TOG labels like moobuzz and Pennywise, conjure images of carefree drinking, perhaps right out of the bottle.

"I find our wine and spirits to be more playful than what's out there. There has been too much stuffiness in the wine business," says Aug.

The Other Guys try to target a price point under fifteen dollars, with a brand identity that speaks to the next generation. It's not a demographic, Aug says, "it's a psychographic." There are a lot of 40 and 50-year-old soccer moms out there buying a twelve dollar bottle of Hey Mambo because they want to feel the young vibe associated with the label.

Over the years, TOG brands have received many accolades. In 2011, Pennywise was rated in the top 100 best buys by

DOMINICAN RUM

KIRK and SWEENEY

• 12 YEAR •

SANTIAGO *De Los* CABALLEROS, D.R.

40% ALC. BY VOL... 80 *proof*
750 ML

Wine Enthusiast Magazine. It also named Leese-Fitch and The White Knight as best buys. In 2012, TOG earned two "Hot Prospect Awards" from *Impact* magazine, the premier magazine within the wine, spirits, and beer industry.

Aug is father to three children: Gabriella, age six, Sofia, age four, one-year-old August III (Gus). They have a fourth child on the way, due in May. Aug's wife, Allison, helps with business events, but both Aug and Allison maintain that "Mom" is her most important title. Aug is protective of his family time and restricts travel and conferences to make sure he reads books to his children before bed. He knows from watching years of family entrepreneurship that there's no line between work and family. So, he adapts. His wife has a mailbox at Aug's office, and she'll often bring lunch to share. As Aug and Allison catch up, they affectionately watch Gus rearrange the office.

"People appreciate my emphasis on family because it's something I encourage them to prioritize, too. Familial relationships are an important part of the human condition," says Aug.

Laptops and Wi-Fi-equipped cell phones allow Aug to spend time with his children individually while touching base with work. Aug likes to show up during lunchtime at one of the girls' classrooms to take them out to get a hot dog. With three children, it's often challenging to focus attention, and this is Aug's way to spend some carefree father–daughter time.

"If everything is going great, my life is quiet and boring. I really consider myself to be a fire extinguisher and the last line of defense," says Aug. "Life doesn't come without its fair share of challenges, and mine is a delicate balance at times." 🍷

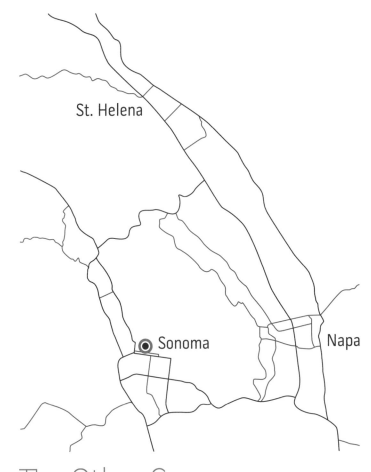

The Other Guys
President: Aug Sebastiani
SONOMA, CA

Established 2004

Known for Leese-Fitch

Plungerhead and Hey Mambo 300,000 case production

100-year history of the Sebastiani family in Sonoma

Also developing spirits and craft beer labels

Aug's brother and sister are partners of TOG

TOGwines.com

Dark Matter

ANGELINA MONDAVI

Angelina Mondavi was born with one of the most distinguished last names in Napa Valley's history, yet it just means "family" to her. When she's not working for iconic winemaker Jayson Woodbridge, she's making wine for Dark Matter, which she owns with her sisters, Alycia, Riana and Giovanna. Although Angelina is a fourth-generation winemaker, she is determined to embrace her individuality and achieve what no Mondavi has yet: a 100-point wine.

■

FOUR SISTERS VINEYARD

Four Sisters Vineyards in Howell Mountain represents Angelina
and her three sisters. Dark Matter Zinfandel is sourced entirely
from its two-acre plot.

Angelina Mondavi, thirty years old and just over five feet tall,
naturally commands. She started working in wine labs at age ten,
moving from washing bottles to pulling barrel samples and making composite blends. By fourteen, she was training incoming
harvest help at Charles Krug, a Peter Mondavi Sr. family winery.
Angelina has just finished her fifteenth harvest, a number
attained by working in both hemispheres.

Angelina hunts for challenges to prove herself—to herself. From
studying chemistry at Villanova University to receiving her
master's in enology from the University of Adelaide's Waite
Campus in southern Australia, Angelina has attained all her success without favor. When she looked at colleges, UC-Davis was
out of the question. "My family's name is written all over [UC]
Davis, and that was the last place I wanted to go."

The Mondavi family has been in the wine business since
Prohibition, when Angelina's great-grandfather, Cesare, and
great-grandmother, Rosa, founded C. Mondavi & Family. Her
great-grandparents set up the company with the intention
of perpetuating the family business for generations, and it's
still in the hands of Angelina's 98-year-old grandfather, Peter
Mondavi Sr., today. Peter Mondavi Sr., along with his two sons,
Marc and Peter Jr., are the owners of C. Mondavi and Family,
which is comprised of Charles Krug, CK Mondavi, Divining Rod
and Aloft.

"My grandfather is extremely passionate about the wine industry.
He can talk day in and day out about everything—from his
research on fermentation to barrel aging techniques. Because I
was surrounded by his passion and excellence, I look for it in my
mentors and in myself," she says.

Angelina inherited her grandfather's passion for wine and works
as an assistant winemaker to Jayson Woodbridge, who has
received multiple perfect scores on his Hundred Acre wines and
is idolized by people in the industry. Angelina is also assistant
winemaker for Hundred Acre's sister brands: Layer Cake, an
everyday wine, and the equally mouthwatering Cherry Pie, a
Pinot Noir brand. It all keeps her busy, and so does Jayson. His
tough but encouraging mentorship nourishes Angelina's promise
as a winemaker and effective leader.

Angelina prefers to work with the best, even if she has to work
harder and take more flak from her bosses. For three years, she
worked as assistant winemaker to Stacy Clark at Pine Ridge
Vineyards, who had worked at the same facility for twenty-five
years. Angelina sees something challenging and interesting
about working with women. Among other things, Angelina
feels her palate is more in tune with other womens'. In
Angelina's master's program, she was grouped with five female
peers, and assigned to create two vintages of wine. She describes their collective feminine style as soft and refined, and
believes this experience provided a foundation for her personal
winemaking style.

In 2010, Angelina left Pine Ridge Vineyards to work for Jayson.
He is her dad's good friend and has been present most of her
life, yet Angelina feels more pressure from him than anyone in
the Mondavi family. Jayson often takes time to sit down with
Angelina for honest feedback. He knows what she needs to
work on and doesn't sugarcoat his comments, but she finds his
honesty inspiring. "He told me, 'You can do whatever you want

"Because I was surrounded
by his passion and excellence,
I look for it in my mentors
and in myself," she says.

in life. But only you can determine whether you're going to be mediocre or the best that you can be.'"

Dark Matter

Angelina practices what Jayson preaches on her Dark Matter wines, a joint venture with her three sisters. Jayson and Angelina's father, Marc, brought the idea of Dark Matter to its tipping point. They reminded Angelina and her sisters that Dark Matter is their chance to make a new name for themselves, beyond what people expect from a Mondavi.

Dark Matter is the liquid equivalent of the sisters' composite values: four generations of traditional methods with a twist. If

Angelina doesn't say much more than that, it's to let Dark Matter retain a bit of mystery. Angelina and her sisters are proud that they learned and grew up with traditional winemaking methods and concepts, but they love to throw in the unexpected. It's dark, and it's sinfully luscious.

"Nothing about this product is orthodox," says Angelina.

The Zinfandel is barrel aged in French oak for four years and then aged in the bottle for about a year. Angelina believes that this long barrel aging is a first for the variety. It's layered with aromatic complexity, ranging from black pepper to lavender. The 2006 vintage, just released and sold out, received 92 points from Robert Parker Jr.

Dark Matter's black label is decorated with a constellation of stars that form a skull. It's edgy—especially for the four endearing Italian sisters. It took years to decide on the packaging, but they had the luxury of four years' waiting time until Dark Matter's first vintage was ready to release. They get a kick out of the shock factor that comes when people see the label, then savor the wine.

To Angelina, enology is not just a convenient career, it's her *life*. It's the unknown—the dark matter—that keeps Angelina up until 2 a.m., only to wake at 5 a.m. for her day job. With grapes, there are constant struggles, questions, and no real answers despite a plethora of available opinions. It takes time to learn the nuances of the land, even when it's just two acres. Angelina doesn't think she'll ever get bored with it, because every vintage presents its challenges.

Within the Zinfandel plot on Howell Mountain, which has been dubbed "Four Sisters," there are several different micro-

climates, and they're all susceptible to different weather. She studies the difference between vineyard blocks that receive morning light and those that receive direct afternoon sun. It affects the wines' acidity. By the time her grapes are barreled, she can taste the distinction in the rockier blocks, and those that have dusty red clay soil. "When I walk through those [clay] blocks, I end up with dust halfway up my leg," she says. Angelina's favorite block is the one that receives morning sun and grows in rockier soil, but every block brings something to the table that is worthy of Dark Matter.

Only about 120 cases of Dark Matter are produced each year, and Angelina intends to maintain its exclusivity. It's sold through a mailing list for 100 dollars per bottle in packs of three.

Angelina is the winemaker of Dark Matter Wines, but her sisters are co-proprietors and are integral parts of this brand. They all have day jobs, but see Dark Matter as a lifelong side project. Alycia, twenty-eight, is mostly responsible for the brand's

marketing, compliance, and shipping. She's also Angelina's roommate. Riana, twenty-five, lives in Seattle, also provides marketing support, as well as feedback when she can. Giovanna, twenty, isn't of legal drinking age, but still weighs in on the bottle and label design and is in charge of social media. "Right now, my sister [Alycia] and I go home and we work on what the next mailer will look like. We're on cloud nine," she glows.

Family Matter

Like many eldest siblings, Angelina feels the most pressure from herself. Slowly, she's learning when to listen and when to ignore her inner critic. There's also the push and pull of being born a Mondavi. She feels there are eyes on her day and night, and the fear of failure always looms. She feels comfort in knowing that if there is a real problem, she can reach out to her family, or mentors.

Despite the constant press about the Mondavis, they are a

notoriously private family. "We're all very protective, and that's the way we like to keep it," says Angelina. In 2008, a 464-page book titled *The House of Mondavi: The Rise and Fall of an American Wine Dynasty* detailed the tragic history of the lifelong feud between Angelina's grandfather, Peter Sr., and his brother, Robert Sr. They never saw eye to eye; Robert was Napa's boisterous promoter, while Peter preferred to research and test his own winemaking practices. However, in the last moments of Robert's life, he and Peter made amends. After years of heartache, the family is connected and content.

Now that the fourth generation has arrived, the two sides of the Mondavi family enjoy each other's company, and work well together. Angelina herself is working on Four Leaf, a project label with her cousin, Robert Mondavi Jr. Still, there are news reports almost monthly that speculate on family feuds and the validity of the Mondavis. A 2012 article claimed that nobody in the family was talking to each other. Angelina laughed at its timing; the week before the article appeared, she had feasted on

"Right now, my sister [Alycia] and I go home and we work on what the
next mailer will look like. We're on cloud nine," she glows.

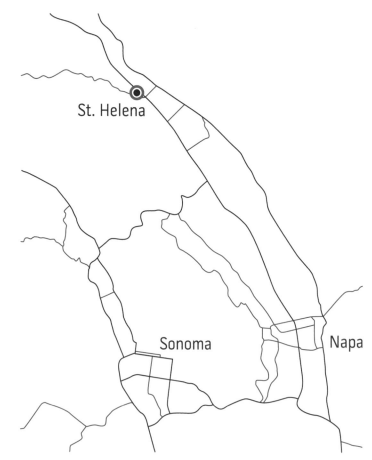

lobster and paella with a few of her cousins. As she likes to say,
"The Mondavis are not going anywhere anytime soon."

With several vintages under her belt, Angelina is able to make
more informed decisions in the vineyard and winery. In 2012,
the vines were extremely productive. Many wineries picked twice
the tonnage of grapes as in 2011, from the same vines. Angelina
is already seeing differences and consistencies between vintages.

"When I'm out in the vineyards, I have to remember the past, see
the present, and visualize the future."

She asks herself questions like, "Do I test nature this year? Do
I pick early, or do I hold onto the grapes? When do I really have
to pull the trigger and pick?" Weather is always an issue. Last
year, Angelina harvested the Zinfandel before the annual rain
started. The year before, she weathered several rainstorms to
let her grapes ripen a bit longer. Rain can compromise the fruit,
especially Zinfandel, which has softer skin than Cabernet. The
decision to harvest is always risky and time sensitive. So far,
Angelina's decisions have worked in her favor.

Angelina is thirsty to absorb the science and artistry of enology,
and Dark Matter Zinfandel is just the beginning of her quest. With
Jayson's mentorship, she continues learning about the subtleties
between grape varietals and the philosophies behind each winemaking decision. In 2011, Angelina added a Cabernet Sauvignon
from Howell Mountain to Dark Matter Wines, though it will be
years until it reaches the market. The sisters purchase this fruit
from their parent's property, Rocky Ridge. Angelina's father
suggests that since Napa Valley is known for its Cabernets, she
has a better chance of gaining recognition.

"This is an opportunity of a lifetime," she says. ⁘

Dark Matter
Winemaker: Angelina Mondavi
HOWELL MOUNTAIN, CA

....

Established 2003

Known for Zinfandel and Cabernet Sauvignon

Grandchild of Peter Mondavi Sr.

Fourth generation winemaker

Started Dark Matter with her three sisters: Alycia,
Riana and Giovanna

Angelina's mentor is winemaker Jayson Woodbridge
of Hundred Acre, Cherry Pie and Layer Cake

....

DarkMatterWines.com

Q&A

Wine on the Web

JAMES PHILIP
CEO and Founder, Lot 18
New York, New York

While playful new labels with entertaining backstories are breaking down the barriers that formed along with the expression "wine snob", Internet companies are facilitating community and encouraging drinkers to expand their palettes.

Social media startup, Likelii, helps consumers discover new wines easier and share their experiences with friends. The site recommends wine to users based on the wines they already like, offers the ability to shop the recommendations, and loops readers into new industry trends from celebrity sommelier Christopher Sawyer. Meanwhile, Lot18, a 50 million dollar flash sales site, provides access to high-quality and hard-to-find wines. Philip James, its founder and CEO, says the Web helps the small winery, while proving that it is the future for buying and selling wine. Philip graciously shares his insights on the industry:

Q: How can the Internet, and Lot18, personalize the wine buying experience?

The Internet can amass data that a wine store cannot. We measure the time a consumer spends on the site, the number of clicks they make, and we take time to understand what each person is like. We ask questions of each member from the moment a person signs up for a Lot18 membership. Trust me, the emails you might get aren't the same as the ones your friend might get. There is a lot of segmentation and carving to optimize the user experience.

Q: How does Lot18 make buying wine easier?

I believe that the Internet provides a better way to buy and sell wine. We offer discounted pricing and increased access to otherwise unreachable brands. And, the delivery and logistics are rather painless for them. We try to educate people who haven't bought anything on the Internet. We don't show every product that's out there and leave it to consumers to make an overwhelmed decision. Instead, we do the work and provide a curated selection that we stand by.

We often look through 15 Chardonnays before we find one we really want. Lot18 showcases very few products for sale each day. We may feature one Chardonnay a day, and we describe why we picked it and what is unique about the winery.

Q: Why do wineries partner with Lot18?

The Internet, and our team in particular, help wineries build their brand and make money through larger distribution channels. We have more than one million members now, which is very attractive to smaller wineries. I have a very good team that travels around the world to explore vineyard stories and wines, so it's not all virtual. The team takes time to understand each winery, and may learn that a particular winery wants to understand how to socially engage new people. We figure out how Lot18 can help them solve their needs, and how can Lot18 solve a larger class of a problem.

Q: What's the hardest thing about being a CEO and how do you address that?

As a company like Lot18 scales, you always have to learn to do something you've never done before. It makes it incredibly hard to train for until you are on the job. As a CEO you are constantly reinventing yourself. You fundraise, then you recruit, then you

manage people. When I founded Snooth, I learned to be a CEO organically. I went from managing 10 people to managing 75, and that was a big unknown time for me. At Lot18, I have investors, mentors and advice givers, but when you're doing something new, you get to a point nobody knows the answer. So, a lot of decisions are based on fragments of information.

My past experiences make the job easier. I've climbed Mt. Everest, which was a genuinely life threatening experience. Lot 18 is still a high stakes game, but comparatively, while the feeling of the unknown is just as strong, people are not going to die if I make a wrong decision. I learn, and won't make the mistake again.

Q: How does social media integrate into your business?

I don't think we've cracked the code. The big question is this: when I buy a bottle of wine and take it to a friends house to be enjoyed with dinner, how can the company get involved in that? We need that social strategy rather than 50,000 Likes on Facebook. We are actively working on it.

CHELSEA PRINCE

Chelsea Prince is author of *Rock and Vine* and publisher of Chelsea Print & Publishing (CP&P). This is her second startup. Chelsea has also worked for Conde Nast, written for a number of startup publications, and has been involved in the non-profit world for a decade. She most recently wrote and published *Snowcial: An Antarctic Social Network Story*, and she currently resides in San Francisco, California.

CHRISTY CANTERBURY, MASTER OF WINE

Christy Canterbury is one of seven female US national Masters of Wine and received the Villa Maria Award for Outstanding Viticulture Examination Paper. Christy is an author, speaker, wine judge and educator based in Manhattan. She has contributed to *Decanter*, *Wine Enthusiast*, Food Arts, *Sommelier Journal*, Snooth, *Beverage Media* and TASTED. Previously, Christy was the national wine director for Smith & Wollensky Restaurant Group and the global beverage director for culinary concepts by Jean-Georges.

MARY STEINBACHER

Mary has seventeen years experience as a photographer – newspaper and landscape. She lives in Napa where she focuses on photographing events, people, vineyards and nature. Her photographs have been used by numerous publications, including magazines and books, National Geographic Books and assignment work for the *New York Times*.

BOOKS FOR GOOD

A portion of your book purchase will be donated to Wine to Water™.
Thank you for your support.

Wine To Water™ is a 501 (c)(3) non-profit organization focused on providing clean water
to people in need around the world. Nearly one billion people in the world today lack access to
adequate water and 2.5 billion people lack access to improved sanitation. Every 20 seconds a
child dies from a water-related disease. Wine To Water is dedicated to countering the epidemic.
For example, the organization distributes water filters in Haiti, Bio-sand filters in Uganda, and
provides wells in Cambodia. Wine To Water™ has worked in Sri Lanka, South Africa, Ethiopia,
Peru, India and Sudan.

Thanks to its readers, Chelsea Print & Publishing has the opportunity to help the cause.

www.winetowater.org